Understanding Your Horse's
EMOTIONS

Discover the facts about the equine mind –
and how to apply them in your day-to-day
management and training

LARRY BENSUSAN

Happy reading best wishes

Larry x

J. A. ALLEN · LONDON

First published in Great Britain in 2012
J. A. Allen
Clerkenwell House
Clerkenwell Green
London ECIR OHT
J. A. Allen is an imprint of Robert Hale Limited
www.allenbooks.co.uk

ISBN 978 0 85131 994 0

British Library Cataloguing in Publication Data
A catalogue record for this book is available from the British Library

Design and typesetting by Paul Saunders
Edited by Jane Lake
Front cover photograph by Debbie Singleton
Printed by Craft Print International Limited, Singapore

CONTENTS

To Amanda Mansell

who gave me the oxygen and the love to write this book

ACKNOWLEDGEMENTS

I would like to thank Claire Shiels who helped me to put my words and various equine researches into a format that has become this book. I would also like to thank Gina Tidy, who two years before writing the book helped me to run seminars on 'Understanding the Emotions of your Horse'; it was from these seminars that the idea of the book was born.

Many of the pictures in this book are of horses that I have had the pleasure to work with. However, I must thank the following people who also supplied some wonderful photographs: Cala Russell, Sarah Roxanne Prentice sarahprenticephotography@hotmail.co.uk, Lucie George luciegeorge@gmail.com and Debbie Singleton www.viewpoint-photographic.com. I also thank the artists who provided the original artwork for, or redrew, some of the illustrations: Jennifer Bell, Maggie Raynor and Carole Vincer.

Lastly, I must thank the scientists whose tireless research on many facets of the horse has allowed us to understand the way of the horse. It is from their research that I have been able to write this book on understanding your horse and our relationship with them. This book is based on facts from their research and my many years working with these magnificent animals, the majestic horse.

chapter one

INSIDE THE MIND OF YOUR HORSE

For around 15,000 years, the horse has been both our friend and co-worker, touching our hearts and sharing a special bond with us. Cave paintings from the Neolithic period show how initially we hunted this animal for food and clothing. Thankfully, for most of us now, this is unthinkable. We have relied on the horse for a variety of purposes over the last few thousand years: for basic food and sustenance in the first instance, to a means of transport, a source of sheer power in agriculture and wartime and finally for our own pleasure and as a means of income today.

This cave painting of a horse from Lascaux, France, is estimated to be 17,300 years old.

Our demands have changed over the centuries, too. Where once we understood him as being a wild animal, harnessing his natural instinct to match our own needs for speed, power and survival, we now often see him as being another child, almost 'human like'. We have of course moved on in our relationship with horses since the Stone Age; from roaming in wild herds and running over long distances to avoid injury or death, our beloved equines are now usually kept in what is our perception of first-class accommodation. Fields providing lush grazing, warm rugs, secure stabling and all manner of accessories, treats and equipment means that the horse has 'never had it so good'. But these things also mean that horses often now stand on their own in a field, fully rugged up and looking dejected. So are we in actual fact kidding ourselves that the horse is better off? Are we treating him with respect, kindness and understanding, or simply denying him his natural instinct and way of life in order to soothe our nurturing feelings and boost our pride?

This extremely important question is the focus of my book. I am not asking you as a horse owner or rider to immediately change your thought process, perceptions, routine and riding technique overnight. Rather simply to open your mind and wonder whether or not it is fair for an animal who has thousands of years of learned responses in him, to be expected to behave in a way that is not necessarily natural to him, but which benefits us personally; conforming to procedures and experiences dictated by us, even though they may be unnatural to, and uncomfortable for, him?

In my experience, despite all the information we have at our disposal – the psychological testing, trials and research that have been carried out over the years – the majority of us are unfortunately continuing to demand more and more from the horse, yet not taking the time to understand or consider his own individual needs. Whether or not this is a case of arrogance, ignorance or simply an unwillingness to delve deeper into the psyche of the horse is a question for debate. What cannot be argued however is the fact that we are commanding this intelligent animal to live in the way in which we think he should, with no regard to his basic needs, psychology or mental health. We do not take the time to try to understand his thought processes, instead choosing to punish him when he does not understand us, or when he appears to be acting in a manner contrary to our wishes.

Translate this to the scenario of the development of the human child. Imagine for instance if, as the child's parents or main carers, we did not allow him to explore his surroundings, regardless of his natural instinct for curiosity. Imagine if he were not provided with or not permitted to play with any toys, and so was given no mental stimulation. Imagine if he was kept apart from other children and so could not socialise. In our society, this would be considered abusive parenting. Yet the horse, who of course sees us as his sole provider of security and nourishment, is simply expected to accept these conditions and no-one thinks any more of it.

The natural horse

Nomadic creatures, in the wild horses will often roam up to 80km (50 miles) per day over a period of around 17 hours (Davidson and Harris, 2002). They spend the majority of their time grazing at leisure and seeking out a variety of grasses not just to feed themselves, but to self-medicate too. As with humans in centuries gone by, before any artificially produced drugs had been produced and we weren't automatically reliant on a pill to help us with any ailment, the horse seems to instinctively know which grass or plant he needs to ensure a healthy diet and to help with a particular minor ailment such as an upset stomach. Whether or not he is born with this ability or whether it is learned from watching older and more experienced horses is unknown. However, whatever climate, vegetation or terrain his surroundings offer him, he has learned to adapt and thrive.

fact

Wild horses self-medicate. They endeavour to stay fit and healthy by grazing on many different plants. Different vegetation offers different or varying amounts of minerals and vitamins.

tip

If you have limited or unvaried grazing space then take your horse to a hedge-line or verge, allow him to graze and carefully observe what the horse selects. This way you will help your horse to stay healthy and you will also gain botanical knowledge along with knowing your horse's physical needs.

Herds of wild horses will either take the form of a harem or bachelor group (Crowell-Davis, 1993). As the name suggests, the harem consists of a number of mares and their young offspring, which will usually all be the product of one dominant stallion – the leader of the herd. Inevitably, there will be a number of young stallions included in the herd at any one time, as they are born and develop. These youngsters are tolerated for some time by the leader, who does not see them as a threat to his status at this early stage. Once they begin to reach sexual maturity however, their behaviour will change. They will become more aggressive, begin to challenge the leader with increasingly violent attacks, and pester the mares. At this point the dominant stallion will simply not permit them to remain within the herd and he will make his feelings plainly and often painfully felt. Unable to compete with the strength and experience of the leader, the young stallions will eventually leave the parental herd to form their own bachelor herd, thus naturally avoiding any problems occurring through interbreeding. Young fillies, although of course no threat to the senior stallion, will also not be expected to stay with the herd and will go on to join other harems or form their own, naturally producing healthy offspring of their own with their new herd. This cycle will repeat itself until the horses either die or grow old when, usurped by younger animals, they are pushed out of the herd to wander alone or in smaller groups until the end of their lives.

These herds have a strict hierarchy and code of behaviour, with troublemakers dealt with quickly and harshly – ideal lessons for young, impressionable horses. Perhaps surprisingly, most horses appear to understand this code instinctively (and should they fail to understand a particular aspect of herd etiquette and make a mistake, the resulting consequences ensure that they learn very quickly not to make that same mistake again). As a result, challenges for leadership aside, herds tend to go about their daily activity relatively peacefully, with each horse knowing their place and deriving a sense of security from that knowledge.

I feel there is much for us to learn here. Although there are unquestionable boundaries and everyone knows who is in charge, instead of feeling oppressed and frustrated, the horses within the herd are comforted by knowing their place and being aware of what is and isn't acceptable behaviour. They seem to realise that living in this type of society is

both a compromise and exchange. Although they must travel where they are told, eat whatever is then available at that location, refrain from bickering and adhere to the senior stallion's wishes, they accept these compromises. In return, they gain comfort from knowing that their welfare is being looked after, they have supportive relationships within the herd and, ultimately, that their survival is ensured, at least for the short term.

Could at least some of these principles be applied to how we communicate with our horses and ask them to perform in a certain way, without physical force? Could we perhaps develop similar relationships to those developed within the herd and tap into this need to be managed, without the use of whips, spurs or harsher bits?

Just as in our society, horses of both sexes will usually form bonds with other horses of the same social standing within their herd, offering friendship, support and learning experiences. These relationships tend to be extremely strong and long lasting. You may not be surprised to learn that these relationships are particularly strong among mares. Women are often highlighted as being able to make friends more easily than men,

Horses have a strict hierarchy and code of behaviour; troublemakers are dealt with quickly and harshly.

Horses together in a pen but take a close look at their faces and see the tension held in the jaws – a sign of stress.

communicate more openly and effectively, show their emotions more easily and form long-lasting, deep bonds. Why this is and whether or not the reasoning is the same for females of other species is a topic of frequent discussion. Whatever the reason, you can see some very obvious examples of existing relationships in a 'herd society' when viewing a small group of horses together in a field on a lazy warm day. Often, they may be dozing quietly together, resting their hind legs, their eyes closed and only the occasional swish of a tail indicating that they are at all aware of what is going on around them. You may see a couple standing head to tail, taking comfort from their physical closeness and keeping flies away from each other or, less often, two horses indulging in a mutual grooming session. As with other animals grooming isn't simply a matter of helping each other out with personal hygiene issues or passing the time. Horses gain a great deal of comfort from grooming by a cherished field or stable mate and couples of either sex will spend many an hour contentedly grooming each other. Again, it is believed that feelings of security and a sense of peace and belonging are to be achieved from such close physical contact from another trusted individual.

fact

Horses are herd animals and many horses find it hard to relax if they cannot see other horses. They are much more reluctant to lie down if they don't have another horse nearby to keep watch for possible danger.

In today's fast-paced, materialistic society, the numbers of people attending counselling continue to increase. Whereas once those who sought external counselling were rightly or wrongly perceived to be 'odd', psychotherapy and counselling is now considered the norm for many people and, in some cases, even fashionable. However, what if, like horses, we were able to easily identify and build relationships with other people? What if by spending time with close friends and allies, talking about our problems or even just enjoying some quiet, peaceful time with them, with no awkwardness or expectation, we could remove the need to discuss painful aspects of our lives with complete strangers? Could simple love, trust and respect for another provide the solution we need? Could the horse actually show us how a simpler life can make for a well-rounded individual?

With foals, although we recognise the importance of bonding with the mother, we often fail to realise that, ideally, he also needs the company of other foals for both learning and socialisation purposes. In the wild, he will begin to wander further away from his mother after only a few weeks and begin to play with other youngsters, finally forming his own peer group or joining another. Although this is an important aspect of the foal's development, of course we don't all have the luxury of being able to allow him to socialise with other foals and mature horses at this stage. Luckily, many breeders will not sell a young foal to a buyer until he is at least eight months old and only after he has run with the herd and learnt how to socialise with other foals and horses.

fact

Young horses who are not socialized with older horses can develop antisocial behaviour.

tip

If you want your youngster to grow into a well-rounded horse then allow him to socialise with older horses, they will be taught invaluable lessons.

Unfortunately, a great number of foals are born into a world where the only source of knowledge is their mother and the humans in their environment. These foals will grow up without having any form of integration or socialisation with other horses and so when they are then placed in a livery yard, they often struggle to settle in. Some become fighters or victims, bullied by their companions and, in many cases, they are simply put in a field by themselves, away from the much needed contact of other horses, once more denied their natural herding instincts. If you want a fully rounded horse, research has shown that it is perhaps not the best thing to breed from your mare, unless you have other foals in your stable. Referring back to my observation earlier, would it be fair to have a child yet not allow him to socialise with other children? How would you expect him to learn? How could he expend that natural, naughty energy of a youngster? Allowing the foal to remain with his mother for a considerable length of time yet not permitting him to socialise with other foals

The natural bonding between mother and foal.

is in complete contrast to what would naturally happen in the wild and so must be very confusing for a young horse.

Mal et al., 1991, observed that young horses, when they are removed from their social groups and stabled alone for the first time, show very obvious signs of stress including loud vocalisation, snorting and pawing. These observations were also noted by Visser et al., 2008, with these behaviours being more pronounced in horses stabled alone than together. After a period of 12 weeks, more than two thirds of these horses had developed repetitive behaviour which we humans consider to be pointless, or even destructive.

Horses can feel
insecure and lonely
if stabled alone.

These results should come as no surprise. For many people, their
sense of security is heightened and their feelings of self-worth strength-
ened in the company of others. Some feel extremely uncomfortable if
they find themselves on their own in their house and will go out to a
friend's home or to the pub. Young women often report that they would
prefer to remain in a bad relationship rather than feel that they were
on their own. Isolation, actual or perceived, is a very real threat to both

humans and some animals, including horses. It is often, particularly in prisons, used as a punishment, such are the dramatic psychological effects it can have on the individual.

Why then, do we feel no guilt or apprehension about stabling a horse on his own? This can be particularly mentally damaging for the animal if he is in a new environment and has been removed from his own herd or social group elsewhere. Surely he must see it as a punishment, frustrated and confused as to what he has done wrong. Feelings of insecurity will often come to the fore, as well as loneliness and boredom. These negative emotions will often communicate themselves as what we perceive to be 'naughty' behaviour. Sometimes aggressive, they are more often to be seen in the symptoms of weaving, crib-biting and kicking.

What most of us don't understand is that a horse isn't born ready simply to be moulded into the animal we want him to be. He has deep-seated instincts and the need to follow the developmental structure laid down by generations of horses before him, a need which in the wild is reinforced by members of his herd no matter their social standing. Just

An angry horse saying, 'go away from me' – but ask yourself why?

because he is now in a domesticated environment, he will not automatically become the equine equivalent of a lap dog. A foal does not arrive in this world desperate to do your bidding, automatically able to understand your commands and accepting of your own human failures. He does not have a wish to perform for you at all times in the specific manner you see fit. Instead, he is likely to live his entire life learning about what it is we want (despite our dreadful, often confusing attempts at communication), fighting against the continuing war between what his instinct tells him and what we instruct him to do. Depriving him of an equine social structure, his basic needs and equine role models, instead imposing our own wishes, expectations and demands, we then tend to blame him when things go wrong. It seems a little unfair, doesn't it?

I have worked with horse and rider partnerships for many years, having had the pleasure of treating everything from family ponies to racehorses. Regardless of whether my 'client' is worth only a few hundred pounds or several hundred thousand, each and every horse is unique in his own way, and they all have a great deal to teach us. Although in many cases, a human client will make contact and ask me to come out and work with their horse to try and improve their performance, they are always amazed when I simply ask them to think more sympathetically not about what *they* need and are asking for, but their horse.

Specialists in horse behaviour like me are often referred to as animal 'whisperers'. To my mind, this now much-used phrase is misleading. I don't communicate with horses on some secret level of transmission, inaccessible to everyone else. I don't have any special gifts and I haven't spent years in the wild, living among herds and becoming an honorary herd member.

What I do have is patience, sympathy and understanding in bucket loads. As a horse owner, I took the time to watch my horses, spend real, quality time with them and build up strong relationships based on trust and respect.

Over time, I came to recognise my horses' subtle (and sometimes not so subtle) signs of how they were feeling. Being able to read them like this can only be gained through spending regular periods of relaxed, peaceful time with your animals, allowing them to act naturally and communicate with you in a trusting environment.

The author aged about three years old on a pony schoolmaster.

Like most of you, I often wondered during these times, what my horses were thinking; what they were seeing, hearing, smelling and feeling. I began to read books and articles by experts in the field of equine psychology and behaviour. Gradually, I began to recognise the signs of tension, depression and boredom in a horse. Just as importantly, as a parent does with their child, I also learned over time to reveal the likely cause of a horse's negative emotions. It was during this time of learning, that I came to realise just how little we really know of our own horse's psyche and how we can unlock the potential of our relationship simply by opening our minds and being willing to learn and adapt.

By understanding the way in which the horse sees the world, we can unlock the key to the door of his emotions and understand what prompts him to do certain things. I am no academic equine psychologist but have worked with all breeds, ages and different types of horses over more years than I care to admit to. Advising clients from the average horsey house-hold to Olympic partnerships, my success speaks for itself. The combined results of my own research and that already carried out by others, form the basis of this book. Like me, you will begin to understand what is really happening within your horse's brain and why he behaves in a certain way which, in turn, will significantly change the way you interact and work with him.

From working with so many different types of horses, I never cease to be amazed by how badly some owners treat them. Let me qualify this statement. Very rarely do I see cases that are ripe for passing to the RSPCA. There are no skeletal horses huddled in the corner of a muddy yard, no corpses lying around, no skinny, lice-ridden brood mares made to produce foal after foal. In the majority of cases, their owners actually adore them and spend thousands of pounds trying to make sure they are comfortable, well fed, look smart and perform well. If I was then to visit their yard and accuse these individuals of making their horses' lives miserable, they would be absolutely devastated. Rather than causing conflict, losing my clients' trust and triggering all kinds of negative emotions, I practise what I preach. Instead, I will think about the horses I have owned in the past and accept that from my own lack of understanding of them at that time, I also did things that I would never do now.

Rarely have I come across a case of undeniable cruelty. In the majority of instances, it is simply that we do not understand what truly makes our horses tick. Rather than feeling regret, however, we can always put a positive slant on our mistakes, ensuring that we can identify them, and learn from them. In my experience, the horse is a very forgiving animal and, provided we are open to learning about him and from him, offer him our understanding and patience and simply try to work on our relationship on that basis, he will meet you halfway and you will notice his behaviour begin to change. In most cases, a horse will not hold a grudge and will be only too pleased to work with you on this new relationship.

Now that, in general, our focus is no longer on simply trying to survive, we humans tend to give considerable amounts of energy instead to our emotions. An intrinsic element of being a human, these emotions, particularly negative ones, can often overwhelm our entire mental facility and interfere with our clear, rational thinking. For example, if you have had an argument with someone at home or at work, this is likely to bring on a bout of anger which will linger long after the argument has reached an unsatisfactory conclusion. One of you will no doubt have turned on your heel and stormed off with a scathing last retort, rather than staying and trying to reach some sort of peaceful ending to the conflict, leaving you frustrated, seething and somewhat irrational. Sound familiar? Have you ever tried to drive when you're consumed by these feelings? I'll freely admit that if I've had a particularly nasty argument or someone has really annoyed me, I'll find myself driving faster than usual, accelerating, braking and changing gear with more aggression than I would normally. My message here is that if you bring this anger with you onto the yard, you are unintentionally transferring that energy to your horses. Unfortunately, however, unlike cars your horses will easily pick up on your tension and I guarantee that it will affect them in some way. Some horses who shy away from conflict may head for the back of the stable in a classic avoidance manoeuvre. Others may become fearful and wary of you, rolling their eyes and refusing to let you take hold of their head collar. Some may even become aggressive in return, sensing your anger as a threat to them.

There have been numerous instances when I have witnessed a horse simply behaving in the natural way horses do, yet being punished because the owner was at that time overcome with a negative emotion. That emotion had absolutely nothing to do with the horse and everything to do with the fact that the owner was unable to control their emotions, was oblivious to the fact that the horse was sensing their frame of mind and was allowing the emotion to override any other thoughts, logical or otherwise, at that specific time.

I remember one yard where there was a very cheeky yearling who was locked in the stable because the fields surrounding the yard were so wet. Being so young, he naturally wanted to be out and playing and so began looking around for something to entertain himself with. By the side of his stable was a drainpipe, with which he took great delight in putting into his mouth and shaking. Of course, the more he shook it the more it moved until the excitement was too much and he eventually pulled the pipe off the wall.

Reading this now and being detached from the situation, I suspect you'd give him top marks for initiative! However, his owner was furious and scolded the yearling, who ran to the back of the stable, unable to comprehend what it was he'd done to make his owner so angry. The drain-pipe was then once again screwed to the wall, an action which the youngster mistakenly interpreted as having been given permission to play again (see what I mean about giving our horses confusing messages?) Within the hour the drainpipe was once more hanging off the wall and this time the owner really hit the roof. The owner began to shout obscenities at the horse, who was still unable to understand what he'd done wrong. After all, hadn't he been given permission to play with the object? However, his owner's anger was very evident to the animal and, fearful of what was about to happen to him, he cowered against the back wall of his stable. In response, furious that the yearling had damaged the drainpipe not once but twice and misreading the horse's reaction as a sign of arrogance and naughtiness, the owner shut the top door of his stable, thus blocking out any light and sources of distraction for the young animal. No doubt the owner was too consumed by anger about the event to think rationally about what the horse may have thought, how their own actions could have been misinterpreted and what result they expected by punishing the horse in this way. No real malice was intended, but both human and animal ended up confused and miserable, simply through a breakdown in communication. If only the owner had walked away, had a cup of coffee and calmed down for half an hour before trying to rationalise what had happened and why, they may have avoided taking further negative action which would only serve to instil a sense of distrust in the yearling, damage their relationship and induce feelings of guilt.

tip

It is important to be calm when working with horses. Assess your state of mind before you start working. If you feel stressed, step away and allow yourself some time to just relax. Remember that horses will pick up your emotions and mirror them back to you.

On another occasion, a horse was on box rest, but found the stable door ajar, whilst his owner was busy mucking it out. Finding the idea of stretching his legs rather attractive after such a long period indoors without much exercise, he naturally trotted out for a spot of exploration, being a curious creature. Upon seeing him, his equine friends greeted him loudly, alerting the owner who, instead of reacting calmly and seeing the funny side of what he was doing before thinking of a plan to recapture him, began screaming at both the horse and her own friends, who came to help. By this time, oblivious to all the unnecessary chaos which was ensuing around him, the horse was trotting happily along the fence line, enjoying this new-found freedom and being able to explore, when he caught sight of a group of women advancing towards him with buckets and head collars. Among the group he spotted his owner and, being a warm, sociable animal, was delighted to see her, no doubt hoping she would play too. Obligingly, he bowed his head to her so she could put his head collar on (now how many of you wish your horses would be as helpful as that?). However, rather than giving him a fond scolding and a pat for coming to her so nicely, once her horse was secured, the owner began shouting at him and jerking the head collar backwards and forwards. This was completely unnecessary – aggressive behaviour no doubt triggered by her fright and anger. However, the horse was naturally confused and upset by his owner's unexpected emotion, not having a clue what he'd done wrong. The result? One frightened horse, who had lost trust in his owner.

So you can see, by understanding the horse's emotions and how our emotional energy can affect his wellbeing and even his competitive performance, we can work on achieving a greater harmony between horse and rider.

If I can give you one message from this book, it is simply to recognise that in an equine : human partnership, the human must be able to put aside their own feelings and needs in order to put the horse's first. Just as we (often reluctantly) as new parents accept that whatever is going on in our own personal lives, we must put that aside when communicating with our child. Marital problems, finance issues, poor health – when we become a parent, our main

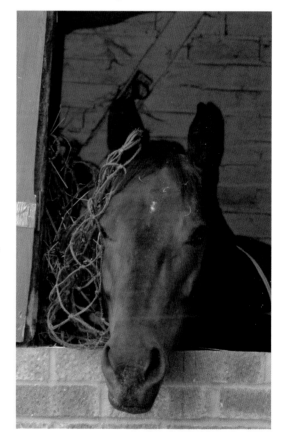

If a horse is feeling content and secure in his environment, the unusual should not worry him: 'Do I look good in this hay net?'

focus must be on the needs of our child. We must shield her from the problems, anxieties and frustrations of being an adult, allow her to grow and develop naturally and behave like the child she is, in order for her to maintain a healthy relationship with us, and grow into a well-rounded individual.

It isn't always easy and most children will at some point find their parent sobbing on the stairs or ranting at the latest telephone bill. Yet dedication, perseverance, consistency and sheer selflessness will always pay off in the end.

It is exactly the same when dealing with your horse. Isn't it worth the effort to ensure that he is happy, mentally balanced and that you understand what he is trying to say to you? Watch his performance really begin to improve, once you have accepted that his needs must always come first. Regardless of bad weather or a raging hangover, make time every day to spend some quality time with him. That doesn't mean mucking out, grooming or any other daily task. It simply means sharing the stable with him for half an hour, talking to him, reading a book or simply pulling your thoughts together. Only by dedicating this time to building your relationship can you hope to be able to listen to and understand what he is saying to you.

Whether you are a trainer, competitor or simply a horse owner, I firmly believe that after reading this book you will not only have a greater perception of the message your horse is trying to communicate to you and a more in-depth knowledge of his psyche and how his own emotions can affect his behaviour, but also your performance as a team will be enhanced through an increase of both trust and mutual understanding. This is not a step-by-step book of recipes for competition success, but simply a book that will hopefully prompt you to start asking questions of your horse and, more importantly, of yourself.

There is no magic cure for the problems you are experiencing with your horse. The answer lies in your own hands and in your ability to be sympathetic, understanding and caring.

Learn how to release your horse's potential, and at the same time, take a good hard look at yourself. Does your horse perform well around others but not with you? Perhaps you are carrying the stress of everyday life with you. Is he sociable with the groom but aggressive towards you?

Perhaps your actions suggest low self-esteem and he feels he needs to be the protecting force.

This won't be an easy journey, but if you are dedicated to making your horse feel as good about himself as possible and releasing every ounce of his potential, then isn't it worth it? Who knows, you may even learn something about yourself along the way.

chapter two

THE DIFFERENCE BETWEEN THE EMOTIONS OF A HORSE AND A HUMAN

I think that as horse owners and/or riders, if we are committed to getting the best from our horses we need to first try and understand the differences that exist between the emotions of a horse and those of a human. As a human, we can create an emotion simply by thinking about it, whether it's a feeling of love, anger, hate, sadness or joy. These emotions can be based on, among other things, events that occurred in the past, or on the situation in which we find ourselves now but, in any event, our senses usually play a large part in triggering our emotions. Regardless of whether we hear something which affects us directly and causes us distress, or we see something on television happening to someone else, which infuriates and upsets us: a story on the news about a child, old person or animal that has been mistreated, for example.

Our emotions tend to be based on experiences and events that have occurred throughout our life and can be stored in our memory. Some of these emotions can be extremely powerful and trigger responses years after the event which initially roused the emotion. This is why I don't personally believe the saying that 'time heals all wounds'.

A horse, however, like most animals, lives only in the present, although in many instances he will learn from past experiences, particularly if they are related to survival. His emotions are less complex and much more basic than those of a human. Instead of fretting over a lost friendship, for example, he will instead be concerned about himself first and his safety. (Although in the wild, every horse within a herd has some responsibility for the safety of the unit, but the overall responsibility for the protection of the herd lies with the dominant stallion and mature mares.) With his safety in mind, it is evident that his emotions will lead to a natural physical reaction to his immediate surroundings. For example, if a horse experiences fear, he will automatically stay and fight or run – commonly known as the 'fight or flight' reaction. Similarly, if he feels anger, he is likely to attack whoever or whatever is annoying him, regardless of whether or not he has a reserved personality. The emotions of the horse therefore are most often simply triggered by his surroundings and the situation he finds himself in at the present time and will lead him to carry out a relevant action. Instincts such as these are often genetically pre-programmed behaviours, which means he was likely born with them and is unable to control their voracity. For example, the first instinct of a newly born foal is to stand and then search for his mother in order to suckle and so to survive. He may receive a little encouragement from the mare, but the instinct is all his own. He doesn't know what he is looking for or indeed even why he needs what he needs. However, once he has suckled, he will associate his mother's teats with a warm, comfortable feeling in his belly and the sense of being protected.

The horse's learning process is divided into two distinct categories: non-associative learning and associative learning.

Non-associative learning

With non-associative learning, the horse becomes accustomed, over time and with repetition, to a particular stimulus. This simply means that he is introduced time and time again to a particular object which has perhaps caused him distress in the past. By exposing the horse continually to the object, he gradually begins to realise that it will not harm him, a process which is used time and time again in training and with horses who have experienced a stressful incident and are therefore fearful of a person, a scenario or an object (Pickett, 2009).

A scenario that may happen more frequently than you might guess is one which is likely to play out on a windy day. A horse becomes terrified when a stray grocery bag flies down the road, blown along by the strong wind, and flattens itself square against his front legs. Not having a deep-seated instinct screaming at us that we should flee from any object which wraps itself around our legs, we can of course think rationally about the situation. In our mind, a plastic bag has flown down the street and is at this moment caught on our horse's legs but it will no doubt blow off again. From the horse's point of view, this could perhaps be a fast-moving, threatening object which is trying to prevent him from running away and he needs to react quickly and violently to prevent himself from being hurt or even killed. It makes absolute sense then for him to throw a complete fit, perhaps rear up, squeal with fear and try his best to run and escape from the danger. From this point forward, the horse may develop what we would consider to be an irrational fear of plastic bags. To him of course, it is completely rational.

An impatient rider would simply believe that their horse was highly strung and adopt a grudging acceptance that a wayward plastic bag would be a real problem forever more. However, a more sensitive, understanding rider might understand exactly what had transpired during the initial traumatic event and how it had affected the horse. Hopefully, the rider would then commit themselves to helping the horse work through his new phobia.

The treatment for this kind of phobia would begin with a slow and gradual process of slowly introducing the horse to plastic bags once more. The first exercise might be perhaps for someone to walk across his path a few feet away carrying a plastic bag. The horse at this stage might well shy away or come to an abrupt halt and stand stock still. Regardless of whether or not he throws an understandable tantrum, he should be brought back to the same place, with the same individual walking backwards and forwards, until he begins to calm down and realise that this bag, although it might still prove a potential threat, is unlikely to attach itself to his legs.

When he has become sufficiently relaxed with this exercise, with the person slowly coming closer each time they walk past, he is probably ready to see the bag close up. The bag should be secured on the ground with a heavy object, in a sheltered spot out of any breeze so that it does not flutter and cannot fly up into the air. The horse should be encouraged to approach it and sniff it repeatedly, processing the information in his own good time that the bag is in fact not a threat.

Only when he appears to have accepted the reality of the situation and seems both calm and confident when confronted with the bag on the ground should it be actually brought to him to sniff. If he is still showing signs of insecurity and fear, persevere with the earlier exercises and move more slowly through them. Eventually, with patience and regular repetition, he will allow a trusted handler to lightly press the bag against his skin, showing absolute trust and confidence that this object is nothing to worry about. This process of repetition and consistent exposure to an object or situation which is causing the fear is a technique known as habituation. The process is considered to be a success when the horse finally accepts the object or situation which would previously have upset him and made him anxious.

An experienced understanding handler can have a positive influence on the emotions of a horse. This horse is being calmed by the owner and is responding by relaxing the muscle on the face and softening of the eyes.

Two happy and calm horses without a care in the world.

This technique can also be used in reverse, when the trainer is asking the horse to increase his response to a stimulus (McGreevy, 2004). This is particularly important when teaching him to recognise the aids of the classical-riding technique. So, in the first instance, we are asking him to put aside his instinct for fight or flight and adopt a calmer attitude towards an object or scenario; and in the latter instance, we want him to respond quickly and accurately to a physical command given by us.

Associative learning

In associative learning, the horse spontaneously learns that something he regularly sees, hears, smells or feels actually means something, which subsequently triggers a reaction in him. A good example is given later in this book where a horse, who had an uneasy relationship with his owner, could identify the individual sound of her car as she drove into the yard, at which point his mood would change immediately and he would become aggressive.

Operant conditioning means that the horse learns he needs to carry out a particular action in order to bring about a reward. If you think about standard animal-training practice, from lions to dogs, the generally accepted method is to reward the animal when he carries out the correct action and behaviour, with a food treat, a technique known as positive reinforcement.

tip

Place a ball or log in the water bucket/trough during the winter and it will stop the water from completely freezing. Horses soon learn to push the object down through the thin ice to get a drink. This is associative learning; they associate pushing the object with getting a drink.

If you think about the basic riding technique, we all know that if the horse is moving too quickly, we need to resist his forward movement a little more by taking our weight back a little and putting slightly more tension on the reins. Although this tension of course doesn't hurt him, this isn't pleasant pressure for the horse but he learns that once he slows down, the pressure will be taken off. This is a superb example of negative reinforcement.

fact

Ponies who were trained with positive reinforcement were more willing to participate in training sessions and showed more curiosity in novel environments than ponies trained with negative reinforcements.

fact

The training in a positive context seems to have a constructive effect on learning and on horse behaviour.

fact

Research suggests that when training horses by either negative reinforcement or positive reinforcement that there was no difference in learning times, but it was discovered that horses trained with negative reinforcement were less calm in training and actually appeared more stressed.

Negative reinforcement should be distinguished from negative experience, however. The latter can mean that a horse has learnt from unpleasant experiences.

In both instances of reinforcement, the horse wins. He is either given a treat, or he is made to feel more comfortable and rewarded with more freedom of movement. This acts as a strong motivational force for him, as he is not being forced to do something – and let's face it, trying to force around 544kg (1,200lb) of horseflesh to do something is pretty much impossible – but is instead being given a choice. A smart horse will learn very quickly how to make the right choice and gain some sort of benefit in return.

fact

Traditionally, many horses are trained by using negative reinforcement, such as sharp pulls on the bit, or the use of spurs or whips to get the rider's desired result. Research has shown that the experiences of a horse during past training can colour, or overshadow, the way a horse views human actions during present training. In other words a horse never forgets his past experiences.

A great example of associative learning however was given in trials (Sappington, B.F. and Goldman, L, 1994) involving four adult Arabian horses. In each trial, the horses were presented with two similar-looking but different panels which they were able to learn how to open themselves, easily. If one particular panel was opened, the horse would find that there was nothing behind it. However, if the other was opened, it revealed a bowl full of food. The location of the panels was regularly swapped around, with results showing that the horses did indeed begin to recognise the individual panel which opened to reveal food. This was the case regardless of its position, giving the researchers cause to even go so far as to suggest that horses could have a problem-solving ability, a suggestion supported by trials held by Hanggi (2003). The results of these trials concluded that horses were even able to solve problems based on the concept of size (i.e. they were able to identify objects which were 'bigger than' or 'smaller than') – exercises used commonly in human nursery schools.

Unbelievable as it may sound, results from earlier trials by Hanggi (2001) seemed to support the theory that some horses can look at a three-dimensional object on a two-dimensional photograph and go on to recognise the actual three-dimensional object from a selection of other objects! Of course research of relevant depth into this area is still in its infancy and it will be interesting to see if these theories can be developed further over the next decade, with further trials exploring the actual capacity of the horse's brain. Regardless of the lack of additional research however, results to date indicate that this kind of problem-solving ability I'm sure, goes far beyond what many of us have traditionally thought to be a horse's typical understanding of his surroundings and mental ability.

We are of course all familiar with a horse's social-learning ability which is present from birth. Both in the wild and in a domesticated environment, given the opportunity to do so, a foal will learn survival and social skills from his mother or from watching other horses interact. Due to lack of research however, experts are as yet unable to pinpoint whether this ability has a strong basis on the foal having any sort of relationship with the horse he is observing or whether social standing in the herd has any sort of influence.

My own feeling is that, if the horse's social-learning ability in any way resembles that of a human, no relationship need be in place. Take for example the 'street' language adopted by teens and young people worldwide. Do they learn this new vocabulary from friends and family? Yes, probably, some of it. However, I would bet that they also pick it up from rap vocals and films. Of course they have no relationship at all with those rap artists and actors, but by adopting the language, it makes them feel as if they belong to a particular social group.

Similarly, with social standing, my own view is that this has no bearing on what the foal learns. If this was transferred to human society, we would then be inferring that formal social etiquette is learned only by the upper classes and landed gentry. This of course is not the case as I have known working-class individuals with the grace and deportment of titled individuals, and wealthy people who have adopted the mannerisms and speech of the working class. Although the class system undoubtedly exists in both our worlds (in that of the equine, 'class' refers to power and authority, which belongs to the lead stallion), I suspect that, as with humans, the foal simply amalgamates all of the information he is able to process about his entire surroundings, the individuals within it and his limited experiences, in an attempt to learn about his place in his own society and what is expected of him in order to survive and thrive.

You may think that there is a world of difference between your beloved horse tucked up in his stable, and the wild herds distributed throughout the world – herds including the brumby horses of Australia, the horses of the Namib Desert, the Sable Island horses in Canada and the mustangs in the USA.

It may surprise you to learn then that these animals are actually descendants of domestic horses (i.e. feral rather than wild), which were at one point turned loose by their owners, or simply strayed. These feral horses have managed to adapt once more to the lifestyle of their ancestors, focusing daily on survival, danger and reproduction – all aspects which play a vital part in ensuring the continuation of the herd.

This then must surely be proof that the domestic horse still retains that strong link to his wild, nomadic past; a link which many of us spend years trying to erase or, at best, dilute or manipulate. Perhaps if we only took the time instead to understand the horse and work with his natural instinct and response mechanisms, our efforts would be more constructive. Surely working in harmony alongside the horse's deeply ingrained abilities and urges, rather than trying to fight and overcome them to our own ends, must be a step in the right direction.

I often wonder if our own horses are in fact any better off than those belonging to the world's herds. In the wild herd environment, the horse is always on the move, looking for sufficient food and water. He lives

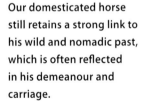

Our domesticated horse still retains a strong link to his wild and nomadic past, which is often reflected in his demeanour and carriage.

constantly with the threat of death either through accident or a predator's attack and so spends most of his waking hours scanning his surroundings for signs of potential danger. He knows his place within the herd and recognises precisely who is in charge of protection.

The domestic horse has many of the same types of worries as his wild cousins and, some might argue, with the lack of a herd's social structure in evidence and dominant protection of the lead stallion, a domestic horse might perhaps even have more concerns. Rather than being able to rely on his own instincts and abilities to satisfy his basic needs, he is often boxed in and has to rely on his owner to provide food, water and shelter, even being deprived of the choice of breeding partners. He is also forced to tolerate his owner's emotions and dominance, or lack of dominance and thus, as he sees it, lack of protection.

Many domestic horses are kept in an unnatural environment. That is they must cope without any other horses for company or protection, remain healthy despite a lack of varied grasses being made available (which would allow the horse, in many instances, to self-medicate) and are forced to behave in the way that we think is appropriate, not necessarily the way in which they would normally behave.

When humans get things right, the equine : human relationship will work: a young horse and a young girl enjoying each other's company.

Surely, looking at the horse's predicament from this angle, it appears that he is really getting a very raw deal from humans. Is it any wonder then that so many horses are now showing very obvious signs of stress, depression and anxiety? Blocking a horse's instinctive reaction can only trigger negative emotions within the animal, emotions which will only be heightened unless we at least try to understand the world from his perspective.

How can we differentiate between instinct and emotion in a horse? In his 'An integrative and functional framework for the study of animal emotion and mood' article, (Michael Mendl, Burman et al., 2010) produced a diagram which showed the relationship between an animal's emotion and mood, which you can see in Figure 1.

In Q1, the horse is highly aroused in a positive way. Perhaps he is excited at returning to his field and seeing his friends, expressing this excitement by giving a few kicks and galloping around for a while, before calming down. We often see this excitement in the hunting field and at

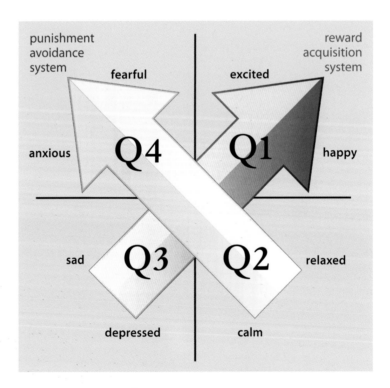

Figure 1. The relationship between an animal's emotion and mood

equestrian events, when the noise of the crowd, presence of other horses and chemicals given off by the rider and the audience can have a significant effect on a horse.

In Q2, he is happy, yet calm and peaceful. We've all seen these horses showing contentment on a hot day, resting in the shade of a big tree with hind leg bent, eyes almost closed and lip quivering. If you often see your horse in this position, rest assured you're doing a good job in making him feel secure, trusting and comfortable. Be wary, however, of confusing this body message with boredom. Provided he has access to other horses and an expanse of field to run around in, then seeing him in this position means all is well in his world.

In Q3, we have the opposite scenario. Here, the horse's arousal is low. He is passive, feeling sadness and even depression. He will often show this by standing at the back of the stable with his head held low. His eyes will have a glazed look about them and his coat will appear dull. The depressed horse will take little interest in his surroundings and needs companionship and stimulation to help him recover his zest for life.

Finally, in Q4, his arousal is high. Perhaps he expects to be punished for something and is fearful or anxious. In this state, he may either bolt, shy, or attack whomever or whatever he perceives is threatening him. A horse in this state is a dangerous animal. He has been taken over by the fight or flight instinct and is somewhat blinkered to anything else or anyone else around him.

Research on rats (Lynn and Brown, 2010) has shown that rats of an adolescent age were more susceptible to anxiety disorders than adult animals. If we transfer this theory to the equine world, it could demonstrate why youngsters are generally more anxious than adults, at least until they begin to learn their role in life and where their place of safety is. Interestingly, it was also found that in animals suffering from anxiety disorders, exercise is an extremely important element in the overall treatment. Can you imagine what it is like for an anxious horse who has little exercise and is only exposed to the walker or is lunged once a day, spending most of his time in his box without real contact with people or horses? If this was transferred to the human world, it would be classed as barbaric, yet we think nothing of treating our horses in this way.

fact

Stabled horses can be more excitable when they are taken out for their daily exercise than those taken out of a field and ridden.

tip

If your stabled horse is jumping with energy and a handful to ride, then turn him out in the field first. Then he can expend some energy in free movement and will be quieter to ride.

Part of the treatment prescribed for depressed humans is exercise. Physical activity releases adrenaline which gives a natural and safe mini 'high'. It also provides the depressed individual with an alternative focus. It is perhaps ironic therefore, that many of us go to such great lengths to find alternative solutions to help our seemingly sluggish horse, when in fact in many instances he knows the exact cure, but is unable to help himself.

I recently visited a yard to treat a five-year-old gelding who, up until the age of four, had been a working stallion. My client, a lovely lady with two children, had bought the gelding several months previously and was delighted with him at first. He appeared to be a calm, friendly animal when he arrived at the yard, and she indulged herself by treating him like another child – a common mistake made by many animal owners. Very quickly however, his behaviour changed dramatically and staff on the yard became increasingly concerned when he repeatedly tried to climb over the stable door. Rather than recognise this attempt as a plea to be allowed out into sunshine and to exercise among other horses, they simply gained the simple impression that this was a problem horse. As a result, they shut the top door of his stable, in an attempt to stop him from causing any damage to them, the stable or himself.

Of course, this restriction of light, vision and stimulation only ex-acerbated the situation and when the horse's owner entered the stable, he terrified her by trying to mount her and drag her by her shirt collar to the back of the stable.

This was obviously a terrifying event which certainly marred any future relationship between the horse and his owner. However, it was very apparent to me that, far from being a vicious, unstable horse, this unfortunate gelding, owing to being treated with kid gloves since his arrival, felt that there was no one in charge and so it was obviously his job to take on the dominance of his 'harem'. Despite his bullish actions, he was in fact extremely confused, anxious and stressed; a melting pot of negative emotions which were only made worse by being shut up in his stable. The poor animal simply wanted to be out and free to enjoy life as a horse.

Out in the open and free to enjoy life as a horse.

Anxiety is one of the most dominant and obvious emotions within a horse, yet as with the yard staff in the last case, we so often misinterpret or ignore it. A moderate level of anxiety shown by the horse on occasion, such as spooking when out hacking or taking a dislike to a particular fence in a competition, is common and to be expected. However, consistent and excessive anxiety will have a prolonged and negative effect on your horse's mental wellbeing.

Horses are great jumpers but if a rider is not balanced then, just like in this picture, the horse is twisted, will land wrongly and may become anxious.

In studies which focused on anxiety in horses (Momozawa, Terada et al., 2007), over 60 Thoroughbred horses aged two were monitored whilst undergoing a series of tests to examine the effect of anxiety on the youngsters.

The tests began in their own stable before the horses were moved to an unfamiliar building, where no other horses could be seen. Eventually, the horses were led to believe that they were completely alone and tethered in this unfamiliar place.

Almost half of the horses of both sexes had broken their restraining ropes and exhibited signs of a significantly increased heart rate within two minutes of being left completely 'alone', suggesting that isolation and unfamiliar surroundings have a profoundly negative effect on these animals.

Let's face it most of us are absolutely abysmal at being able to hide our emotions. However, some people are able to 'put a brave face on it' or 'laugh through the tears' and so sometimes their emotions can go unrecognised. However, to the trained eye, strongly felt emotions do in fact cause us to make subtle changes in facial expressions, brain activity and heart rate. These fluctuations form the basis for lie detector tests and so can be measured, which helps researchers with their studies in psychology and behaviour.

fact

There is some evidence that a nervous handler affects a horse's behaviour. The handler's heart rate can affect the horse's heart rate in situations that can be difficult, such as when loading.

Emotions in both humans and animals occur in response to situations in which we feel we will be rewarded or punished for something – for animals, rewards include food, water, shelter and companionship, and punishments include physical attack, discomfort or even hurt. Reward and punishment therefore lie at the heart of all emotional states and determine whether they are positive or negative. (Lang et al., 1990; Gray 1994; Cacioppo et al., 1999; Watson et al., 1999; Carver, 2001; Rolls, 2005; Barrett et al., 2007; Nesse and Ellsworth 2009).

Physical sensations picked up by the senses and communicated to the brain can also be associated with reward or punishment. For example, if you give your horse a mint, he will normally pick up on the pleasant taste, which in turn will make him happy. He will then associate the mint with this happy state, which will make him want more of them. Unfortunately, many of us know from experience that food awards can lead to a horse pestering you for the same treat every time he sees you. We then become annoyed and punish him for searching for the treat, a punishment which is totally confusing for the horse who then feels rejection and is disconcerted by this negative response from his owner.

If however, a horse frequently finds himself in what he feels to be a potentially threatening environment (if there is a kennel of constantly barking dogs next to his stable for example), he may come to believe that he could be attacked at any time, and develop an ongoing high state of negative arousal. This of course would mean he would be perceived by us as a potentially dangerous and aggressive horse. Alternatively, if he is able to avoid the stress of being surrounded by potential threats for most of the time, or is generally kept in a safe environment, a low arousal, positive mood state may be maintained.

If your horse is kept in an environment in which he lacks for nothing and feels safe by being secure within his 'herd' and having his owner as his protector, his mood is likely to be well balanced and amiable. On the other hand, an animal who feels insecure and whose needs are consistently not met will likely become sad and depressed over time, particularly if he is provided with little stimulation, no routine and lack of compassion from his human carers. This can often happen in full-livery yards, where the grooms simply carry out their job, neglect to interact with the horses and don't turn them out.

What I would like to stress right here and now is that your horse's needs are just that – the needs of a horse, rather than *your* needs. You may think that keeping your horse safe in a stable day after day, making him wear any number of rugs and lovingly plaiting his mane is the epitome of horse husbandry. I disagree. Think of him as the animal he is, how he would behave and what his needs would be if he was in the wild. Over the years, I have seen symptoms of depression in many stabled horses, particularly those who have been on box rest for several weeks, whilst horses out in the field can often be seen galloping around at play with other horses, obviously happy and excited.

For those animals who have been unfortunate enough to have experienced a significant traumatic experience, post traumatic stress disorder (PTSD) is likely to only magnify their emotions.

In studies carried out on rats (Hendriksen, Prins et al., 2010), the effects of enriching the environment for the animals, who were also given the option of undertaking voluntary exercise, were evaluated and discussed for those animals which were suffering from PTSD. Ten weeks after being exposed to the trauma, the rats displayed a reluctance

right Horses can demonstrate their dominance through play, this way no one gets hurt.

below Horses love to play and are inquisitive.

to move about in the open. Even antidepressant drugs had little effect. However, although environmental enrichment (which included introducing a shelter, a secure 'nesting bag' and stimulating activities) introduced before the trauma took place did not prevent the animals from exhibiting signs of shock afterwards, when it was implemented either immediately after the shock or one week later, it was shown to help the rats make a complete recovery, three weeks after the trauma.

A running wheel was also added, so that the rats suffering from shock could undertake some voluntary exercise and this was proven to reduce anxiety in the animals.

So what do these results mean? Well, in humans, depressed and anxious people are often advised to take up an exercise programme if they are able to. Although antidepressants will no doubt assist them with their recovery, many people with this problem have found additional support through regular exercise. This is no surprise, as we have known for years that adrenaline, the 'feel good' hormone and a change of focus can bring about significant results in such individuals.

With horses, it tells us that stressed, depressed or anxious horses are more likely to respond well to a calm, safe environment, preferably with other horses around to act as stimulants and perceived protectors. Regular exercise will also give your horse something else to think about, with the released hormones during work giving him a 'feel good' boost.

fact

Animal studies have shown the importance of physical exercise in the treatment of post-traumatic stress disorders and the recovery from anxiety disorders.

tip

If you have an anxious horse, ask yourself if you are giving him enough quality exercise.

Many emotions demonstrated by a horse are luckily very evident and clearly communicated – to those of us who know what to look for. All you need to do is be able to understand what triggers a particular emotion in your own horse so that, within the partnership, your relationship can grow and trust develops between the two of you. This will result in a happy horse and owner, and for those of you who compete, a better performance.

chapter three

UNDERSTANDING THE CHARACTER BEHIND THE EMOTIONS

Having worked with horses over a number of years, I have come across many wonderful characters; from the calm, relaxed and laid-back hack to the fiery, dominant and powerful thoroughbred. To understand more about these very different characters and their emotions, we need to delve further inside the horse's brain and examine how even a domesticated pony maintains close links to his wild ancestors in the form of instinct, as well as think about how we as owners and riders can tap into this instinct to get the best from our equine : human partnership.

Initially, many people thought – perhaps with a degree of arrogance – that the horse's brain was very small; around the size of a walnut in fact. It was believed that horses had no memory and simply acted on pure instinct. Why this was so, I have no idea as it seems very obvious that a horse can remember at the very least other animals, and individual humans as well as routine. If he were to have no memory, why would he whicker when he sees his favourite human and how would he be able to remember what he had been taught in the schooling ring? Regardless of this, we now know, through extensive research, that this is most certainly not the case and that the horse does have a considerable memory, although the function of his brain primarily seems to be focused on controlling his muscle coordination, balance and body functions.

What you may not realise is that the horse's short-term memory is slightly more delayed than that of a human, meaning that when you give an instruction that he has not come across before during a lesson or schooling session, it is unlikely he will be able to process the information and respond to your request immediately. This may seem like he is resistant to the instruction at first, but horses learn best through repetition and he will eventually begin to associate cues from certain movements made by you as the rider or from the sound of your voice. Once this information has been understood and reaffirmed through positive reinforcement from you, then it will be stored and you'll notice that he begins to respond to that particular instruction more quickly and accurately.

This is a problem often encountered during training. We give a command and expect the horse to obey us immediately. When he does not (because his brain is still processing the information), we interpret this as disobedience and become angry, often punishing him through harsh contact through the reins or with our heels, or even using the whip on him. This negative behaviour will not help in the slightest. On the contrary, your horse will become confused through not understanding why he is being punished, frustrated and probably downright angry. And who can blame him?

fact

According to research, what a horse learns on his left side isn't necessarily learned on the right, and vice versa.

tip

When training or handling your horse, if you want him to learn or understand something new you must carry out the task on both sides before the horse will absorb the information.

Tests which were carried out on horses (Hanggi and Ingersoll, 2009) to uncover the actual time it took for them to process information, revealed that given an unfamiliar and complex instruction, the horses could quite easily make up to 150 mistakes on average over a period of time, before they were able to process the information effectively, began to actually understand what was required of them and so learn the lesson. The more the horse practised the task, the fewer mistakes he eventually made.

Similar tasks were requested of monkeys for the same purpose. Bearing in mind that monkeys are similar to humans in many ways you would expect that they would be able to understand and carry out the instructions correctly in a much shorter space of time than the horses were able to manage. In actual fact, the monkeys required on average nearly 700 repetitions before they began to learn the lesson.

Putting that into context then, we have for generations expected the horse (whom, you will recall, we thought had a tiny brain) to understand our communication immediately and comply much faster than an animal who is so similar to man. The fact that we have expected him to think in the same way as we do, therefore, does seem somewhat contradictory, don't you agree?

Although it may take a horse slightly longer than we might anticipate to process information, he has shown that his brain power is formidable within the realm of the animal world. It is also generally accepted that he does have an excellent memory. Tests carried out by Marinier and Alexander, 1994, involved a number of horses placed into a maze, at the centre of which was a reward in the form of food. The tests revealed that once the horses had managed to negotiate the maze, they had an amazing sense of recall and could find their way to the food, even when tested again two months later; a remarkable achievement even for a human.

We should use this information and incorporate it into our technique when training a horse. Patience, understanding and consistent repetition is much more likely to bring faster, better results than if we demand instant, impossible compliance and reward the horse's temporary confusion with punishment. Remember that your request is virtually impossible for a horse to satisfy immediately, but he will usually be trying to understand you so give him time and repeat the request each time you school him. Your persistence will pay off in the end if you work with the

- This horse lacks confidence and will shy at anything from a wheelie bin to a small piece of paper. It will take considerable time and patience to walk past a newly painted gate which yesterday was green but today has been painted white. In our logical brain, we know it is the same gate despite its change in colour, but to the horse, who thinks in terms of pictures rather than objects, that gate was not there yesterday, so he will naturally be fearful of it. In some ways, he has the same thought pattern as an autistic child.

- A right-side dominant horse can be very distrustful if a stranger walks into his stable, displaying his distrust by snorting and possibly moving to the back of the stable with his hindquarters facing the stranger, ready to defend himself if needed.

A right-side dominant horse, as we have learned, still feels the emotions and reacts to the instinct of his cousins in the wild. He is therefore best ridden by an experienced person who understands his personality and recognises that he requires patience, support and reassurance, not punishment. In most cases, although his behaviour can seem erratic and alarming at times, no harm is ever intended to the human. He needs someone who is prepared to spend significant amounts of time with him – not training and not carrying out stable duties, but just being around him – and who is patient enough to gradually allow significant trust to develop over time, which will help his nervousness immeasurably.

The left-side dominant horse

The left-sided brain horse, although usually a more logical thinker, tends to be very dominant and will often try to throw his weight around, pushing you around and sometimes even pinning you to the wall if he feels you do not have enough dominance to protect 'the herd'.

He is very confident and playful which, inevitably in this instance, can indeed lead to naughty behaviour. This behaviour should be carefully monitored to understand individual situations and whether the horse is actually behaving in a naughty fashion, or is just misunderstanding you.

This horse is reminding the crowd that he is number one!

The way in which your horse kicks is a great way of identifying which type of horse you have. A left-sided brain horse will line you up first, so that he can be sure his hoof will actually connect with you when he does kick. Because he is so confident that he would win hands down in a fight with you, he will not run away afterwards but will stand his ground. This is therefore one of the most dangerous types of horses to have around. Conversely, a right-sided brain horse will kick out in your general direction and then run away immediately to avoid any negative reaction and

Some horses are more left-brain dominant like these confident and calm horses showing all the characteristics of left-brain dominance.

punishment from you. He is acting on pure instinct and his intention is not to hurt you, but to warn you off.

Many left-side dominant horses are actually lazy and stubborn, preferring mental stimulation rather than having to do a substantial amount of physical work. Your horse may well simply want to go out and play with his friends in the field rather than be forced to learn lessons and will, like a small child, have a temper tantrum or even just lie down, which of course is very disconcerting, particularly if you are seated on him at the time! Similarly, rather than graciously accepting a mint as a treat, being food-orientated he will bully you for more. Unless a treat is being given as a reward for specific training, the feeding of treats should of course always be avoided as it can lead to pestering at the very least and even biting, one of a horse's particularly nasty traits.

fact

Humans often prefer using their left or right hand – horses can be the same with their legs.

tip

To find out whether your horse prefers his left or right side, watch the side he usually lies down on, or the leg he strikes out with when angry.

tip

The Lipizzaner stallions at the Spanish Riding School in Vienna, Austria, receive one small hand-fed treat after each training session. Horses learn quickly to look forward to a reward – but remember, treat only for specific training, not just when you feel like giving.

Although we've all seen horses bucking through excitement, with the left-sided horse it can indicate a lack of confidence or confusion about the instruction you are giving.

For generations, we have attempted to breed horses who think with the left side of their brain, i.e. more logical horses able to dampen down their instinct and perform well, unlike their predominantly right-sided brain cousins. However, we then become annoyed when we feel the horse is being naughty and is ignoring our instructions, essentially asking him to think less for himself and simply do as he is told.

The thinking function with this type of horse is so logical that he can memorise the movements required in a particular dressage test, which seems fantastic at first until you need to move onto the next test and he becomes frustrated and fights against you, believing that you are doing it wrong.

Unfortunately, we can't have it both ways!

In many horses, as with humans, we will see typical characteristics which stem from both sides of the brain. This is the ideal, striking an equilibrium which will both calm and balance horse and rider.

Take a look at Figure 2 (see page 56) and plot whether your horse is more right- or left-sided, or indeed whether you feel he is actually neutral. Once you have identified this, you can take the first step towards becoming a more sympathetic and effective rider or owner, basing your technique on maximising the more favourable characteristics and playing down his more negative behaviour.

tip

If you were buying a dressage horse, or one for cutting work (working cow horse) then ambidexterity would be helpful. Buyers of these horses would be well advised to spend time watching the horses as they stand – this can be very helpful in identifying animals that are free from a significant left or right bias. If a horse constantly rests one leg in preference to the other, this could show that it favours that leg and would not, therefore, be easy to train for some disciplines.

Supporting the right-sided brain horse

This horse, as we have discovered, can be nervous of the unknown or unfamiliar, and so will relish being in a stable he knows well, in an environment he is sure that is safe. If he can live among other horses, this will help him immensely, supporting the feeling that he is being protected. Routine is also very helpful in ensuring he settles in, being aware of his social status within the 'herd' and taking comfort from knowing exactly what is happening at any given time.

The smallest diversion from routine or unexpected event can upset him, so when working around your horses, be constantly thinking of anything which could cause an emotional upset or any potentially stressful situations. For example, make sure that this horse's stable is not the one next to the feed room, as when he sees buckets being filled with food and carried past him, he may well begin to fret in case he will be left out. He's a sensitive soul! Alternatively of course, you can simply feed him first so he knows that all is well with the world and will leave you in peace to feed everyone else.

a.

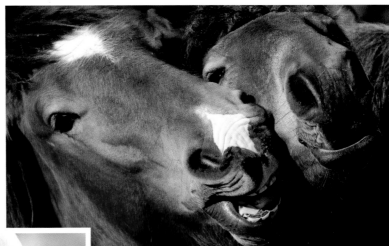

Character traits: a. As part of their individual characters, horses can show many facial and emotional expressions; b. The droopy lip reveals that a horse is totally relaxed and at one with his surroundings; c. It is more likely that a foal who has bonded with his mother and is confident of his place in the herd will have a stable character: mother stands watch over her new foal.

b.

c.

When out riding or training, and your horse shies or bolts away from an object which he thinks is threatening (and this of course could be anything from a leaf blown around by the wind to a bucket), the worst thing you can do is to pressurise him into going and having a proper look at the object. Although repetition works with many horses, this must be matched with sensitivity and understanding. Kicking or using your riding whip to force him into another approach will make him feel extra pressure in addition to the already existent fear, and he is likely to go into complete meltdown. Instead, ask him to go forward just a little and then retreat repeatedly, the moment you feel his nervousness begin to take over. This tactic of going back and forward will of course demand considerable patience but by doing so, your horse will begin to trust your judgement and understand you, therefore gradually becoming more confident. Eventually, he will become surer that the object is not a threat and that it is safe to pass. This is a much more long-term solution to nervousness, enhancing your relationship and building a solid foundation for the future.

Remember that your horse is unable to understand commands immediately, and will need a little thinking time in order to process the information you're giving him, so don't expect to see immediate results. If you are both relatively calm and you have asked him to do something, you will be able to tell if he is trying to understand you and is considering your request, by the way in which he licks his lips. Think of him as a human who sticks his tongue out the side of his mouth when he is concentrating!

Remember too that this type of horse will look to you for assurance and security, so if you are a nervous rider, you are both likely to end up with your nerves in tatters. A relationship built on mutual wariness and insecurity is no relationship at all.

These horses need owners who are calm and dominant yet kind in order for them to feel secure and happy. An ideal owner would be someone who the horse perceives to be a leader of the herd, a protector. If you are about to buy your first horse, then this type of animal is definitely not for you. He will recognise instantly that you are a novice and will understand that you are unable to give him the security he needs. Unfortunately, I often see first-horse owners investing immediately in a highly strung animal such as a former racehorse. These types of horses often have strong right brain tendencies and will become increasingly fiery and indeed a nervous wreck, once they realise that their new owner is as nervous as they are.

In the hands of a competent, experienced owner, this type of horse can develop and perform out of his skin in a discipline such as eventing or dressage. However, paired with a novice, there usually lies years of heartbreak, anger and frustration ahead on both sides. This is highly unlikely to be a mutually supportive partnership and may well result in disaster.

fact

Heightened flight response is more desirable in racing breeds than in horses used by riding schools or as draught animals. Keep this in mind if you buy a former racehorse as a riding horse.

Supporting the left-sided brain horse

If you have a left-sided brain horse, you should expect to spend a considerable amount of time with him, making sure that he has enough mental stimulation to entertain that clever brain of his.

Unlike the right-sided brain horse who relies on routine to make him feel safe, this type of horse is usually excellent at coping with varying terrains and surroundings. If he is instead kept in a stable all day with little interaction, you can expect him to develop behavioural problems.

Research has shown that dressage horses currently stand head and shoulders above the rest when it comes to displaying behavioural problems. It has been suggested that this is because, although dressage is a complicated discipline, it can be somewhat repetitive and the left-sided brain horse will become bored very quickly, yearning for fun and adventure instead. In the past, many dressage horses were only ever brought out of their stable to be placed in the walker, or to practise tests. Now, thankfully, many of the top dressage riders have recognised the need for variety in work and environment and give their horses different activities to keep their brain engaged, including jumping or long hacks in the countryside.

In one specific dressage yard, a lady would only buy her horses from a number of yards in Holland to ensure they had excellent blood-

This horse is a three-day eventer, who gets lots of variety in his life and variety is the key to a happy horse.

lines. Although these horses were always renowned for their competitive ability, once in her hands their performance consistently seemed to drop. This was not because she was a bad rider, but because the horses had little stimulation other than constant dressage practice. The constant repetitive exercise resulted in her horses' brains switching off and in the end their performance suffered. This is why variety of work is so important if you want to get the best out of your horse. As a left-sided brain horse is food-orientated, you can use his compulsion to your advantage when working. For example, if you are in a jumping lesson and he performs well, why not reward him with a leisurely massage and some of his favourite food? Gradually, he will then begin to associate this treatment with performing well over jumps, and be eager to perform well for you each time, for the treat which lies in wait at the end of it.

This type of horse (or indeed any horse for that matter) should never be left alone day after day in a stable or he is likely to become depressed and withdraw into himself.

Research carried out by Martine Hausberger et al., 2009, and Hanggi, 2009, revealed that when comparing left-sided brain horses who had access to open areas for grazing to those kept principally in stalls, the more restricted horses were the ones who showed signs of bad behaviour.

This is a strong message that in order to maintain a happy and obedient horse, he needs to be allowed to socialise and to be stimulated.

In my experience, I have found that some owners who train their horses in a particular discipline such as dressage expect them to refrain from showing any equine emotion. This, in addition to restricting their natural movement, places undue pressure on the animal who will often respond by indulging in negative behaviour including cribbing, weaving and head shaking. Horses who are being trained in more natural, physical disciplines such as jumping or eventing however, can also display negative behaviour if they are not permitted to behave in their own natural way, although these horses tend to prefer more repressive licking or biting of various natural objects.

These types of activities are often seen in foals weaned in unsuitable conditions, and can signify problems even this early in their development.

Having to carry out constant repetitive exercises often makes the left-sided brain horse dull, bored and uninterested in their work, regardless of whether they are an eventer or a dressage horse and you will often see the horse begin to demonstrate symptoms of psychological problems. So, if you have a left-sided brain horse, teach him new movements and disciplines regularly and don't just practise the same thing on a daily basis. Be creative and have fun, and your horse will have fun right alongside you.

Common negative behaviour

We have all seen horses who engage in repetitive, annoying activity. However, rather than trying to understand why the animal is doing this, often we simply buy tools to try and repress the behaviour.

One of the most common symptoms of an uncomfortable horse is consistent tongue play with the bit, which is often an attempt to avoid the pressure that the bit causes in his mouth. This pressure can in fact cause damage to the trigeminal nerve in the horse's mouth, which leads to constant head shaking, which in turn can be exacerbated by either a strong hand or a piece of tack pulling the horse's head down.

Because the head is often forced down during dressage, you will find that many dressage horses show symptoms of head shaking and nodding.

The head being forced down is a type of restraint that can lead to neck pains and stiff muscles, which of course will affect the horse's willingness to perform well and cause him unnecessary stress and suffering.

If you think your horse could be suffering as a result of his surroundings or miscommunication between the two of you, why not try to interpret his behaviour for yourself and adjust the way in which you are working with him before consulting a horse trainer or changing the tack? It can sometimes be difficult to look at ourselves in an attempt to help our horses, but you may find that it can be a great deal less expensive and considerably more effective. It could be that simply by 'being' with your horse and spending quality time together, ensuring he is safe and allowing him to indulge in his natural 'herd' behaviour, you will see significant results and a happier horse.

fact

Research has shown that large stable mirrors have a 67 per cent success rate of reducing unwanted behaviour because, if horses feel isolated, a mirror gives them comfort.

Try becoming a human **being** around your horse, not a human **doer**. Many of us, as a result of work, children or lifestyle, become human doers around our horses. We go to the stable, lunge, perhaps ride, muck out, change the rug, check the water, feed them and pat them before locking the stable doors and driving off home to complete the next chore. This routine is often repeated day after day with the poor horses receiving no stimulation or bonding with you, eventually showing their displeasure by adopting behavioural problems. I reiterate my advice to you: stop just doing and start being!

It is important to be a human being not a human doer; this horse has a relaxed face as his owner thanks him for a good day's work.

chapter four

FIGHT OR FLIGHT: THE SURVIVAL FACTOR

We humans are a demanding lot and we have demanded a lot from the horse. Indeed, we continue to try and erase the horse's innate impulse to run at the first sight of trouble for our own ends. Ever eager to please, the horse will attempt to comply with our wishes but, every so often, his own DNA will override even our most strenuous request and the sensitive horse owner should understand this reaction and attempt to pacify and instil confidence in their horse, rather than punish him.

Most horse owners will have heard of the concept of fight or flight in wild horses – but do you know precisely what it is and are you aware of how this can relate to, and affect, your domestic horse?

In the wild, a herd of horses will when threatened quickly assess the danger, decide immediately whether they stand a chance of winning a fight with this particular predator or challenger, and act instinctively. This process can take just seconds to work through, being more instinctive than logical. Unlike humans, horses do not utilise logic. This is because they have not developed the frontal cortex area in the brain which is found in humans and, because they have not developed this brain function, horses have little or no ability to plan ahead, consider events or visualise in the mind's eye. Instead their behaviour is controlled by responses learned previously by trial and error.

fact

Horses use all their senses to investigate their world and during investigation they tend to be very alert, excitable and ready to flee at any hint of danger.

So what exactly is this mechanism of fight or flight? It is simply a series of psychological changes which take place within the body, in direct response to a particular situation. The adrenaline hormone is secreted, the blood pressure elevated, the heartbeat accelerates and the muscles tense up, ready for the animal to take action immediately on the basis of their decision.

With adrenaline levels raised, these two horses are in the fight or flight mode

Thousands of years ago it was the same for humans of course: we lived off experience and wits, and mortal danger will have presented itself every day during our fight for survival. Our instincts were just as sharp as the horse's then but in our modern era we fortunately have less need of them, and so we are no longer affected by the fight or flight instinct. Or are we?

Imagine that you are out shopping in a quiet part of town when you are confronted with a tough-looking thug who demands your rings. One was given to you by your husband and the other belonged to your mother, who sadly passed away last year. Both rings are therefore of immense sentimental value. The instinctive part of your being will quickly assess and balance the anger you have towards this threatening person against the likelihood of you being seriously hurt should you fight back. Should you struggle, or simply run for the safety of nearby busy streets?

Believe it or not, a more usual scenario for fight or flight amongst humans can actually be found in the workplace, or even at home. Stress in these environments can trigger symptoms of fight or flight, including raised blood pressure. Over the longer term, these can bring about the physical symptoms of which we are seeing more and more in today's societies: symptoms including arthritis, irritable bowel syndrome and ulcers. Some of these conditions can be triggered by our constant inability to act upon our fight or flight instinct – after all, we can hardly run away from home or simply get up and leave our office.

It is the same for horses. Studies have shown that, when threatened, those horses that choose the flight option tend to run for about four miles before stopping to take a breath and reassess their surroundings. Unfortunately, most of us don't possess fields that large, so our horses in this instance are stuck; unable to give into their instinct and run for the preferred distance, causing even greater fear, stress and anxiety.

fact

Although a horse's first response to the unfamiliar is flight, his second response is usually curiosity.

Equine stress and tension

You may never have considered the possibility that your horse is suffering from a considerable amount of stress. It is a real possibility, and one which has been proven, time and time again.

For example, a stud farm I used to visit would regularly test the sperm count of every stallion as part of its quality control process. Over time, it became apparent that for some reason, the sperm of some stallions that were renowned for producing excellent offspring would be inexplicably low. Eventually it was discovered that if a stallion was given a nervous handler at the time of testing, more often than not that particular stallion's sperm count tended to be considerably lower.

This demonstrated how effectively horses can pick up on our human energies and emotions, indicating that if we are stressed, it is likely that our horse will become stressed too, simply through our direct contact with him.

Pain and discomfort

I have also often noticed that horses suffering from anxiety and stress tend to be affected by pain or tight muscles, too. How many of you suffer from either frequent or infrequent headaches as a result of built-up tension in your neck and shoulders – a direct result of consistent stress? Horses are also prone to aches, pains and stiffness for the same reason. To their way of thinking, however, these ailments can truly mean the difference between life and death.

There are a number of studies that have examined humans who are suffering from chronic aches and pains, and the effect of this constant discomfort on their overall mood and disposition. In one study, 70 per cent of those involved who were suffering from constant pain expressed feelings of anger. However, until recently, there had been little research into how the same can affect horses.

Carole Fureix PhD, of the University of Rennes, agreed that there was a need to identify this link in horses, saying: 'Several studies have implicated that experiencing acute pain can affect the social behaviour of humans and animals in that the risk of exhibiting aggressive or violent behaviour is increased'. Along with a number of colleagues, she set about trying to develop this theory further, supported by clinical evidence, resulting in the revealing article, 'Partners with bad temper: reject or cure? A study of chronic pain and aggression in horses.' 2010.

In total 59 horses were used in the trials: 44 geldings and 15 mares, all aged between 5 and 20 years old, most of whom were French Saddlebreds. The horses underwent several tests and were subsequently assessed by an equine chiropractor, to find out if they were experiencing back pain.

The results were startling. An astounding 73 per cent of the horses were suffering problems of the vertebrae, mainly in the areas of the croup, withers to mid-back, neck, and mid-back to croup.

Over 75 per cent of the horses showed signs of aggression and overall negative behaviour towards the humans involved in the trials by putting their ears flat back, stretching their neck and threatening to bite.

It appears then that there is indeed a direct connection between a horse who regularly shows aggression, and chronic discomfort.

But what does this mean for the owner or handler? Well, before you punish your horse for showing aggression to you, why not stop and think about why he might be acting in this way? Could it be that you feel angry yourself and you are transmitting these feelings to your horse? Or could he be in considerable pain? Think about how you react to others when you are in pain or unwell. Rather than trying to forge ahead with building an uneasy connection with your horse founded on mistrust, pain and anger, you could try to identify the problem, understand why he feels this way, help him to correct it and work on building a stronger bond built on peace, understanding and trust. As Ms Fureix states: 'Human awareness of this association may well alter the perception humans have of "bad tempered" animals. Chronic pain should not be overlooked as a cause of aggression in horses.'

Having the fight or flight mechanism firmly engrained in a horse's DNA means that should a predator attack, his instinct tells him that, if injured in any way, he would not be able to flee as quickly as usual. A horse suffering in this way will therefore plough all his efforts not only into disguising his disability (so that any potential predators will not be able to pick up on his weakness and will therefore be less likely to attack) but also into avoiding any perceived danger as much as possible. This makes the horse more anxious than usual and you will see him begin to shy at objects and situations which would, in the past, not have worried him at all. If this is happening to your horse, try running your hands over his body and feel if he has any telltale knots of tension, which you can massage away. Don't be fooled into investing in expensive gadgets; none of them will be as effective as the touch of your gentle hands. Alternatively, I find that using a tennis ball works just as well.

hint

A horse that stands in the field all week and then is ridden for hours on a weekend is a prime candidate for lameness.

tip

If your muscles are sore after your ride, your horse's back and legs are probably sore too – so give your horse a massage after the ride!

It is possible to use the fight or flight mechanism to our advantage; with police horses the mechanism is utilised for controlling crowds.

By regularly massaging away any areas of tension, you should visibly see your horse begin to calm down and relax. A big sigh, that quivering lip, closing eyelids or a rested hind leg are all signs that he is content and feels safe. Now is the time to begin work and you should see notable changes in his behaviour.

In many yards, horses tend to graze in fields alone, without any companionship to help them feel calmer and more secure. They are therefore deprived of important social grooming which is known to be an important aspect of stress relief within the equine world. We take away their protection and ask them to repress their natural instincts yet fail to replace them with soothing hands-on massage (vibrating rugs are *not* a suitable substitute) or thorough grooming.

above **Mutual grooming is a necessity for a horse's well being; it is thought that it releases natural endorphins.**

right **The top lip curled in this way is often seen during mutual grooming or when you rub a particular area such as the withers.**

Have you noticed, whilst grooming your horse, that he sometimes becomes extremely agitated at the feel of the brush on his coat, and will quiver when it touches certain areas? He may also try to avoid the saddle or bite you when you are fastening the girth. These are sure signs that he has either injured himself, that the saddle does not fit correctly or that the girth is rubbing his skin, making him extremely uncomfortable. Try not to become impatient or angry with him during the grooming process if he tries to move away, flinches or reaches round with the intention of nipping – how else is he meant to tell you it hurts?

tip

If your horse becomes uncharacteristically grumpy or starts to bite you then perhaps he is in pain, or not feeling well, and doesn't want to be messed with. Run your hands all over your horse's body and see if he flinches or moves away from you. You could also take the horse's temperature.

Discomfort around the withers or girth region

Try to massage any area where you feel that there may be tension, particularly where the saddle and girth lie. Also include the areas that twitch when being brushed. As suggested before, use a tennis ball, which fits easily in the hand and does a great job in deep-massaging muscles. I guarantee the horse will think it feels great.

fact

Vigorous grooming around the withers of a horse will produce a drop in heart rate and produces a pleasurable and relaxing response.

If, after you've carried out a considerable massaging session, you are still experiencing problems around the withers or girth area then contact your saddler. It may well be that your saddle simply needs reflocking. If the saddler feels all is well then check to see if your horse could have perhaps injured himself and is in fact complaining that the saddle is irritating the injury. Massage could well be the answer in this case. For a rubbing girth, give the skin a few days to heal and then use a different type and length of girth. Always be ready to at least try to be open to whatever your horse is trying to tell you. Ignoring the problem will not make it go away but will inevitably make it worse.

fact

A Swiss study on race-training saddles, saddles with traditional wooden trees, flexible synthetic trees, or no tree at all, found that all the saddles gave high-peak pressure during most gaits but there was more pressure on the back during trot. However, out of the saddles tested, a treeless saddle showed a higher-level pressure point on a horse's back than the flexible tree.

Rugging

Horses are often kept in fields offering little or no protection from the sun, rain or cold. In years gone by, when horses were part of everyday life: business, work and pleasure, if no natural shelters were available, man-made shelters were thought to be absolutely necessary when keeping a horse outdoors. Now, however, many of us prefer simply to use a rug instead. In the summer, the animals should be rug free and will be content to be so, although many horse owners choose to follow the current fashion and subject their animals to fly rugs and head masks. In the winter, the cycle of clipping and rugs begins again, increasing the horse's stress levels.

Summer has come but this horse is covered with fly rugs and a food restrictor, which all raise the possibility of vitamin D deficiency.

fact

In the winter, the horse grows a woolly coat to keep warm in the colder temperatures. It is then shed in preparation for the summer. However, a horse's hair does have other functions: it protects against predatory insects and is a pathway for the transportation of pheromones and other physiological signals from the body in relation to protection. Personally, I wonder if clipping both winter and summer can reduce a horse's insect protection.

fact

Many owners are giving their horses additional stress in the summer by rugging them with flysheets to stop the flies biting; studies have shown that vitamin B1 (thiamine) is known to provide insect repellence.

tip

Give your horse brewer's yeast which is high in vitamin B1 to help stop fly irritation – it may also help with sweet itch and will improve coat condition.

fact

Horses can stand in deep snow; their lower limbs and hooves almost never suffer from damage due to the cold. This is because the legs below the knees and hocks are made up of mostly bones, tendons and tissues that don't freeze easily. In extreme cold temperatures, blood-shunting mechanisms in the hooves alter circulation patterns to preserve body warmth.

During a discussion I once had with a German trainer, he expressed his astonishment at the British practice of clipping our horses and then covering them with ill-fitting rugs in winter, repressing their free movement. He quite rightly pointed out that the horse's winter coat is there to keep him warm. Of course, when we take his rug off to ride out, in his clipped state he is therefore essentially naked. Becoming sweaty and then rapidly cooling down in this state means he is therefore extremely vulnerable to the cold.

fact

A natural coated/unclipped horse can adapt to temperatures as low as -15 °C (5 °F) before he must increase metabolic heat to maintain normal body temperature. The upper critical temperature is believed to be between 20–30 °C (68–86 °F) before he must lower his body temperature, usually by dilating blood vessels in the skin, sweating and/or panting.

Unclipped horses can adapt to low temperatures of up to -15 °C and can usually maintain their natural warmth when playing in the snow.

I have often seen horses scraping their teeth along the wall or biting at wood, or indeed their owner, as they have a rug placed on them. We interpret this behaviour as naughtiness rather than recognising the stress we are placing our horse under by covering him with this artificial 'blanket'.

One of my clients had literally dozens of rugs for her horse: 36 to be exact. Where on earth did she store them, I hear you ask? Believe it or not, she built an extension onto her house, specifically for that purpose.

Another client worried constantly in the colder months that her horse would be shivering, so would put six rugs on him at a time, to try and keep him warm. She was oblivious to the fact that he could hardly walk and felt sore around his neck.

Neither of these clients was intentionally cruel to their horse. It was obvious in both instances that they absolutely adored their animals but simply did not comprehend what it was that their horse actually needed. They were projecting their own emotions, fears and stress onto the horses, unconsciously using them for their own needs.

In the first instance, the lady saw her horse almost as a fashion accessory, much in the same way as a girl will dress up her dolls, or a wealthy person will buy expensive collars and outfits for their dog. She was determined that her horse would want for nothing – whereas in fact, what the horse really wanted was simply to be a horse.

In the second case, the lady had a strong nurturing instinct; honourable, yet confused. Her instinct was to protect her horse in the way she would a human child, who would undoubtedly feel the cold without the benefit of layers of clothing or blankets. Her horse, however, obviously had different needs and this confusion led to his pain and suffering.

How to tell if you are over-rugging your horse

The easiest way to tell if you have over-rugged your horse is to put one hand under the rug and the other on the parts of your horse's skin which are not covered by a rug. If the hand that is under the rug feels really warm whilst your other hand is much cooler then you may have over-rugged him. The difference between the two areas should only be very slight, not considerable. A more accurate gauge can be given by taking your horse's temperature.

Vitamin D and sunlight

Tests have proven that horses who are rugged all year round can suffer from a deficiency in vitamin D which is of course obtained partly from different foods and from the sun's rays. Vitamin D is needed to maintain calcium levels and absorb phosphorus effectively. A deficiency will often lead to increased nervousness, painful muscle spasms, leg cramps and numbness, with bone malformations as a result of softening bones occurring in extreme cases. I have heard of many owners buying artificial supplements and calming products in an attempt to help their horses, when in fact all they need is *at least* ten minutes of sunlight on their bare back on a daily basis, particularly in the winter, when sunlight is in short supply in the UK.

Physiological signs of stress

How can you tell if a horse is suffering from stress and if his system is functioning normally? As I go around my clients' yards treating horses, I am amazed by how many owners have no idea of how to look for the signs that there is something not right with their horse. They often can tell that an animal is below par when being ridden but have no idea what to observe before getting on board.

There are a number of things which can affect the health of a horse and his emotions. These can often be seen by a change in behaviour or condition on the outside, but you should also consider what may be going on inside the horse which may trigger those symptoms. Do you for example know what your horse's heart rate, respiratory rate or temperature is at rest? From discussions with a number of horse owners, I found that around 80 per cent simply do not have a clue.

If you measure your horse's pulse rate, respiration rate and temperature regularly, you will soon learn what is normal and will therefore be able to tell quickly if something is amiss.

Taking a horse's temperature

A horse's body temperature should usually be between 99–101 °F (37.8–38.3 °C). Up to three degrees either side is acceptable. Your horse will be obviously warmer in the summer, during or immediately after exercise or when he is stressed or excited. However, even when rugged, his temperature should not exceed these guidelines. If it does, then you may have over-rugged him or he may have a fever. Of course, if you suspect he is ill, contact your vet immediately.

It may sound odd, but always attach a string to the end of the thermometer to avoid losing the instrument altogether – it happens! If using an older thermometer, ensure that you shake down the mercury first; plastic digital thermometers are also very effective.

Make sure someone who is confident, quiet and calm is holding the horse. Lubricate the tip of the thermometer with Vaseline or saliva, move the horse's tail to the side and insert the thermometer gently into the horse's rectum, angling it slightly towards the ground. Most horses are unlikely to feel uncomfortable but be sure to avoid any flying hooves if this isn't the case with your horse. To obtain the most accurate reading, leave the thermometer in place for at least three minutes. Once you have taken the reading, clean the thermometer thoroughly, preferably washing and wiping it with antiseptic before returning it to its case.

Taking your horse's pulse

Measure your horse's pulse rate in the morning, afternoon and at night. Compare it with the pulse rate after he has cooled down after work and after eating. In this way, you will start to learn more about both your horse's emotional and physical condition.

The pulse rate of an adult horse at rest averages 25–40 beats per minute (bpm). A pulse rate of 50 or higher in an adult horse at rest may indicate a problem. The average pulse rates for young horses are 70–120 bpm for foals, 45–60 bpm for yearlings and 40–50 bpm for two-year-olds.

The horse's pulse rate will increase if he is excited or nervous, in pain, during or after exercise, or if he is unwell. As a general rule of thumb, the higher the heart rate of the horse, the more severe the condition.

The pulse can be taken by feeling the heartbeat through your horse's chest wall just behind his elbow, or on his backside, just either side of the dock. However, the usual area for taking his pulse is under the left side of the lower jaw bone (mandible) where you will feel a major artery. Using your forefinger so that you don't pick up your own pulse, press against this artery firmly. Use a watch or stopwatch to time a 15-second period (remembering that two quick thumps in succession count as one beat). Then, multiply the number of beats you counted by four to arrive at an accurate reading.

How to check a horse's respiration rate

The average respiration rate of an adult horse at rest is between 10–15 breaths per minute. This increases in hot or humid weather, during and following exercise, or when the horse has a fever or is in pain. If he is breathing rapidly even though he is resting, you should contact your vet immediately. Check that he is spending the same amount of time inhaling as he is exhaling, and that his respiration rate is not faster than his pulse rate.

Watch or feel your horse's ribcage and stomach for one minute then count the number of times he breathes over a 60-second period, counting one inhale and exhale as one breath. If you are having difficulty seeing the ribcage move, watch his nostrils instead or place your hand over them to feel him exhale.

For a more accurate indication of his respiration rate, a stethoscope is needed, which you should place against his windpipe (your vet will show you how to use one). In this way, you will also be able to hear if it is being blocked by mucus.

Identifying gut sounds

Another great indication of possible illness is the sound your horse's gut makes: it should always be making noises. If when you listen to the gut there is no noise, this often means that there is a problem and you should contact your vet; a complete lack of sound is often an indication of colic.

Press your ear or, even better, place a stethoscope against your horse's side, just behind his last rib. You should be able to hear gurgling noises, which would indicate that his gut is working correctly. Remember to check both sides.

How to check for dehydration

Healthy horses should drink a minimum of five gallons of water each day. If your horse refuses to drink water, try adding a sugar-free flavoured drink such as apple juice to it to encourage him. If this doesn't work, contact your vet after a day or two. Don't let him become dehydrated, which can be extremely dangerous.

If you're not sure if he's drinking enough, gently pinch a fold of skin on his neck. If it goes back to place almost immediately, this would indicate that he's fine at the moment, although you should keep any eye on things for a few days. If after being pinched the skin stays wrinkled, call the vet out immediately.

Checking a horse's mucous membranes

A horse's eyelids, gums and the inside of his nostrils are lined with mucous membranes. By checking that they are of a normal colour, you can see whether there could be a problem with his blood circulation. The gums of a horse with a healthy circulation are pastel pink; slightly paler than those of a human. However, if they are very pale, bright red, greyish blue or bright yellow, you'll need to call a vet.

These warning signs indicate:

very pale pink – potential fever, blood loss or anaemia

bright red – possible poisoning or mild shock

grey or blue – severe shock, depression and illness

bright yellow – potential liver problem.

Unfortunately, rather than helping a horse to get well, some modern vets actually add to a horse's stress. Whereas in the past, diagnosis and prescription would have been mainly carried out on the yard, horses who are injured or ill, and insured, are now often boxed up and taken to the vet's practice, away from their familiar environment, to be given test after test, scanned or even put into an artificial coma to find out the cause of their illness. Don't you find this ironic, given the level of stress that it causes the animal if the problem is 'minor' – and preventable – and could be treated on the yard? With a serious problem, of course, this may be the only way to get the horse the correct treatment.

As I visit yards on a daily basis, I am now seeing increasing numbers of horses suffering from arthritis, ulcers, laminitis and colic, all of which can be stress related. The message is simple. We need to stop being selfish and imposing our own dreams, needs and demands upon our horses. We also need to educate ourselves in the way our horses think and behave, understanding their true needs and ensuring that we meet them. To avoid doing so, once we have the information to carry this out, is nothing short of cruel.

In their article 'Could Work Be a Source of Behavioural Disorders? A Study in Horses' (Hausberger, Gautier et al., 2009), the authors highlighted the results of research which indicate that various types of work in particular demand significant suppression of emotion by the horse. This suppression is directly linked to stress which, if sustained indefinitely, may lead to adverse effects on the horse's health.

Dressage training in particular was identified as requesting particularly unnatural responses from the horse, which could bring about substantial levels of stress. This discipline often demands a constrained gait and forced curved head carriage which not only prevents the horse from being able to move his head freely and check for any threat, but can also lead to physical damage. In tests carried out on a number of horses, von Borstel, Duncan et al. revealed that the extreme neck curving in some areas of dressage resulted in significantly more tail swishing, mouth opening and symptoms of fear than was shown in other horses.

This is not to say, however, that all stress is negative. Recent research carried out by French, Austrian and German scientists has revealed that a moderate amount of stress, as with humans, can actually prove to be beneficial to horses.

By measuring the levels of cortisone in horses' saliva both before and after a potentially stressful situation, it was revealed by Christine Aurich, professor at the Graf Lehndorff Institute and the University of Veterinary Sciences in Vienna, that their levels of stress do indeed rise considerably, but fall rapidly once they have performed.

The scenarios used as the basis for these tests included presentation for sale and classical dressage and show-jumping competitions. In all scenarios except the competitions, the horses' cortisol levels returned to the same level as before the event within approximately an hour. After competitions however, their stress levels did reduce but had not returned to their pre-event level even after two hours.

Aurich was keen to point out, however, that in all cases stress levels were not as high as with young horses undergoing initial training, transportation and those castrated or undergoing colic surgery.

As might be expected, stress levels were markedly lower for older and more experienced horses who had been through the same scenario time and again, and therefore whose perception of potential threat was lessened.

The combination of stress at work and added stress at rest – perhaps tension between a group of horses kept in the field together or a lack of interaction and stimulation, can not only be detrimental to a horse's health, but can eventually define his behaviour.

Rolling is a good way for horses to release stress and they must be allowed the room to perform this enjoyable activity.

Behavioural manifestations of stress

A horse under stress will often appear apathetic and uninterested, or perform repetitive negative actions including weaving, cribbing, windsucking, head shaking or tongue playing.

Cribbing

It is not known exactly why a horse might first begin to show signs of crib-bing but many find it a means of entertainment during an otherwise very boring day standing alone in a stable. Solitary confinement is thought to be a contributing factor but there may also be links to genetics, too.

A horse who consistently crib-bites will lock his top incisors on an edge, usually the top of his stable door, or a beam. He will tense his neck muscles and make sounds akin to swallowing great quantities of air. As this is an apparently addictive activity, many horses come to prefer crib-bing to exercising, socialising or even eating.

A cribbing horse finding comfort on the post despite wearing an anti-cribbing strap.

Radiographic studies have proved, however, that the horse is not in fact swallowing air, despite the sounds he makes. Instead, the air inhaled is forced into the top of the oesophagus and then exhaled into the back of the throat. Unlike cribbers, horses that wind suck don't need to grasp an object to perform this act.

Horses that spend a great deal of time cribbing can lose weight and condition, particularly if their obsession with this activity is stronger than the impulse to eat. They may eventually develop unusually heavy neck muscles and grind their teeth down. There may also be evidence to suggest that it can trigger a higher incidence of colic too, due to going for long periods without food and then bolting down a large feed offered by a worried owner. One study that focused on the transit of food through the digestive tract showed that a longer digestion period was required by consistent cribbers than by non-cribbing horses fed in a similar manner.

tip

To reduce boredom and digestive problems, feed stabled horses – particularly those with a tendency towards cribbing and weaving – small, frequent meals, rather than one large meal.

Another feeding study discovered that meals containing grain tended to increase the amount of cribbing activity, whereas meals containing pelleted alfalfa did not. It is therefore suggested that food stuffs containing higher fat levels such as rice bran, or super fibres, the most common of which are beet pulp and soy hulls, may be a useful alternative when feeding cribbers. These feeds are more digestible than traditional fibre sources and great for older horses too.

It is not only the stomach that can be negatively affected in cribbers, however. In a study of 14 horses, a mixture of cribbers and non-cribbers, the heart rate amongst the cribbers was shown to be higher than in the other horses; a rate which appeared to decrease when they actively indulged in the activity, suggesting it is a soothing mechanism, much like smoking in humans. These horses tended to be more highly strung, responding much faster and dramatically to frightening stimuli outside their stables and refusing to rest. This could suggest that cribbing is a more deep-seated problem, related to stereotypes and a nervous disposition, an idea supported by studies which have found that some individual family lines contain a much higher percentage of cribbers than others.

Many owners, in an attempt to stop this problem, use a cribbing strap which fits tightly around the horse's neck behind his jaw, which prevents him from flexing his neck muscles. Some have even resorted to surgery, having the associated nerves and muscle tissue removed. However, with this procedure, it was shown in a trial that 12 out of 30 horses continued to find a way to crib-bite, despite the surgery.

Weaving

Similarly, horses who consistently engage in weaving can damage their health as a result of focusing more on weaving than on exercising and eating.

A weaver will tellingly shift his weight from side to side, swinging his head and shoulders. As this is more commonly found in stabled horses, it is thought to be a reaction to boredom and lack of stimulation and can, in extreme cases, lead to stress on the legs and hooves, and wear on the shoes.

A horse can sometimes be physically prevented from weaving by installing bars within the stall or above a stable door to prevent this movement. However, both cribbing and weaving are obviously a means of coping with stress for the horse, and so by removing their means of self-soothing, we will evidently increase their stress levels even more. It is therefore much more effective to prevent rather than treat the problem by ensuring your horse receives as much time in the field as possible with his group of friends and avoiding stressful situations such as isolation and boredom. Existing nervous habits can also be reduced by employing this strategy. If turning your horse out is not possible, make sure he has a companion stabled alongside him in addition to some stable toys such as a ball or items hung from the ceiling.

These negative patterns of behaviour, observed by Cooper and McGreevy, 2002, affect between 10 and 40 per cent of stabled horses and are thought to be connected to a combination of the feeding of low-fibre or high-grain content feeds with only restricted time to indulge in the horse's normal social behaviour.

Some horses may show signs of stress more obviously than others. If you suspect that your horse is not feeling well, or is feeling stressed, you can often tell by a rise in his temperature, so by learning how to take his temperature or check his pulse (see pages 82 and 83), you may be able to understand him more accurately. Iridology, studying the iris of the eye (the coloured part of the eye), can often yield answers too, although this is something I will go into in greater depth later in the book.

Unfortunately, far from understanding the plight of the horse and trying to address the underlying issue behind his negative behaviour, some of us merely try to correct it using a combination of unnatural and often stressful techniques including electric shock treatment and even surgery. We are often afraid that by simply allowing the horse to mix with other horses and permitting him to just be a horse, he will encourage the other horses to behave in the same negative manner; and so we continue to keep him isolated. Treating the symptoms rather than the cause is unlikely to lead to a successful result. Indeed, it can often make the situation worse and the horse even more depressed and stressed.

Not everyone has the benefit of extensive land and a number of horses, allowing normal socialising behaviour, which is a horse's birthright. If you must stable your horse on his own, you may find that a foraging device, which releases pellets on the floor as the horse pushes it around, encourages him to forage for food which he would do normally in the wild. Thorne et al., 2005, suggests that a number of such devices, requiring the horse to forage more often and for longer periods, will distract him and help to reduce his negative behaviour.

Goodwin et al., 2005, however, urged a note of caution when using these devices. With devices placed on the floor, it was argued, there was the chance that the horse could also consume foreign bodies as well as the pellets. In addition, in their trials, all horses were successful in finally retrieving some food but differing devices meant that it could often take some time in order to do so, which led the horses to show signs of frustration.

Another suggestion was given by Cooper et al., 2000. Their trials showed that episodes of weaving were significantly reduced by providing stabled horses with a clear view out of their box and a grill separating the stables, rather than a solid wall, so that the animals could at least feel close to each other and interact, even if their top stable door was shut. They achieved outstanding results with this theory, reporting that no weaving at all was shown by any of the 10 horses in the trial (half of whom had weaved for at least two years) when they had clear views from the front, back and into each other's stables.

fact

A study found that weaving was significantly reduced by providing stabled horses with additional fields of view, including a grilled opening between adjacent stables.

Never underestimate the power of fight or flight within the horse. Equally, you should be sensitive to the varying signs of stress that your horse may be exhibiting in response to being unable to fulfil this instinct. It is presumptuous of us to expect the horse to understand our communication and instruction without taking the time and effort to learn his language and take into account his needs and basest nature.

Research by Rivera et al., 2002, and Sondergaard and Laedwig, 2004, showed that horses kept out in the field in social groups tended to perform better in training and were less aggressive on the whole than those horses who were predominantly stabled. This of course makes absolute sense in both the equine and human world. If you are, overall, contented, not stressed and interested in what is going on around you, you are much more inclined to want to learn and so will be able to process information much more easily and effectively. If, however, you feel repressed, distracted, depressed and isolated, it is unlikely that your mind will be open to learning new things.

In many ways, the psychology of the horse is no different from ours. Imagine how you would feel if you were kept in a room all day with nothing to look at outside but a bare wall. Imagine if you were not allowed to socialise with other people and if you were given the same thing to eat, day after day. That is precisely how many of us are treating our horses, yet expecting them to be happy and perform well for us. Is it any wonder then that negative behaviours begin to develop quickly? It is simply the horse's way of expressing himself and providing at least some distraction from his boring, lonely life.

chapter five

LOOKING AT THE WORLD
AS THE HORSE SEES IT

As humans, our emotions are heavily influenced by all our senses. Hearing a familiar song can instantly trigger memories of a particularly happy or sad time; smelling a scent on a person as they pass by on the street can remind us of a loved one; most memories and emotions are linked in some way and can be brought abruptly to the surface by one or more of our senses.

Sight

Sight and emotion

Our eyes in particular are a key trigger for an emotional response. Imagine, for example, you saw an old lady being mugged across the street. No doubt you'd immediately feel anger and outrage, with the initial reaction of fury caused by what you have just seen leading you to make one of two decisions. If the emotion was stronger than a logical consideration of what could happen, you might become involved. How many heroic people have you heard saying 'I didn't stop to think' after risking their lives to save someone else? But, had you been more logical and thought prudently about what might have happened to you if you had intervened, you would most likely call the police.

Alternatively, picture a mother holding her newborn baby and smile at the warm and tender feelings which arise as a result. One very popular print which has been the favourite of women for many years is the one of a man holding a newborn baby in his hand and gazing at it. Seeing images of babies and animals can for many people trigger an immediate maternal or paternal instinct, an instinct which, in the wild, would prove crucial to the survival of the family or herd.

Advertisers have long since recognised the link between sight and emotions, using gorgeous models to promote scent and beauty products; cute animals to promote everything from toilet tissue to tea bags and, most recently, shocking simulations of children involved in traffic accidents to warn drivers of the danger of speeding.

You might think that horses, having spent thousands of years in the wild, would have superb eyesight. And to a certain extent, that is true. For example, how often whilst out hacking, has your horse suddenly stopped dead with a tense body, pricked up his ears and flared his nostrils and, if you tried to speak to him, flicked his ears momentarily back to you, before flicking them forward again to focus on the source of his attention? You, wondering what on earth he'd seen, peered into the distance

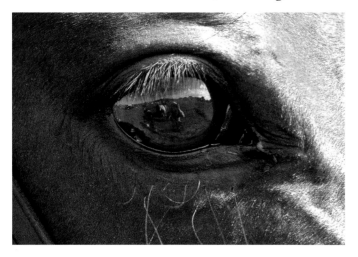

Looking at the world as a horse sees it.

yet saw nothing. Then, gradually, you perhaps noticed a small rabbit hopping along the hedgerow towards you, or a group of walkers heading your way. As they came closer, your horse seemed visibly relaxed and put his nose down to sniff the new arrivals, or began to walk forward again. This example shows that horses do not just rely on sight but also use sound and smell to pick up danger or, as in this example, a group of walkers.

Types of vision

For humans, 20 : 20 vision, although not perfect, is classed as being perfect, meaning that we can clearly see the details of an object from 20ft (6m) away. For us to experience what the horse sees, we would need to stand 30ft (9m) away from the object when its details would not be so clear to our eyes.

The horse is unable to see static objects from as far off as we can. However, he has the remarkable ability to see any movement far into the distance, often long before we are able to pick up on it. This of course makes perfect sense to the horse in the wild, who may not necessarily need to be able to see a rock in the distance, but certainly does need to be able to see a potential predator stalking the herd, from as far away as possible. This then gives the herd the best chance of escape.

Equine vision is designed to target moving objects at a distance.

Because a horse's eyes are set on either side of his head giving him an enviable almost 360-degree vision, nature has designed his eyesight accordingly, which unfortunately means that he does, as most riders know, have blind spots, where he is either unable to see at all or where his vision is severely limited and lacks clarity. These blind spots mean your horse will be unable to see anything directly in front of him any closer than 4ft (1m) away, or directly behind his tail. For this reason, it is always advisable to approach a horse from the side, talking to him and letting him know you are there, rather than risk startling him and being on the receiving end of a sharp hoof, as a result. Bear in mind too whilst grooming or working around him that he can lose track of you as you move around, crossing into and moving out of his blind spots (Figure 3). He will not comprehend that you are still there and that you haven't left, so any sudden movement as you move back into his line of vision can startle him.

There are some blind spots but horses have nearly 360 degrees of vision enabling them to see predators both in front and behind them.

Best area of sight

Blind spot

Blind spot

Objects may be blurred

Figure 3. Blind spots
(illustration by Maggie Raynor)

The horse's eye has two main functions. Firstly, as we've just discussed, it will pick up any signs of movement, particularly across long distances, which is of course particularly useful for horses in the wild who are constantly on the lookout for danger. A horizontal strip set in the centre of the eye will concentrate on the object in question. Because the horse has blind spots (see Figure 3), to compensate for this he will lower his head and raise it to eliminate those blind spots bringing the object into focus so he can then decide whether it poses a potential threat. This is why you will often see your horse raising or lowering his head when he is interested in something; he is simply trying to achieve a greater understanding of what it is he is seeing.

It is the term 'binocular vision' which is our description of the way in which a horse can see moving objects both from the side and at the front, over a considerable distance (Figure 4). Not only that, he can also use each eye independently to see each side, right around to his hindquarters, an ability known as 'monocular vision'. With monocular vision, be aware that the horse will not see as we do, his vision being two dimensional, whereas we see objects in '3-D'. He can see three-dimensional objects, however, when he looks straight forward with his binocular vision. He is unable to use both types of vision at the same time, but usually favours binocular, choosing to investigate situations and objects by looking forward. You will best see this demonstrated when he lowers his head to examine something lying on the ground and sniffs it to be able to try and identify it.

To translate this into a riding scenario, remember that a horse is most comfortable when he has the option of being able to use his binocular or

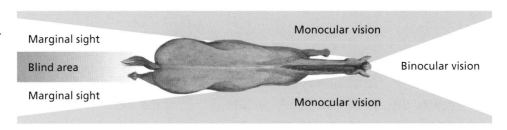

**Figure 4.
Monocular
and binocular
vision**
(diagram by
Carole Vincer)

monocular vision whenever he needs to. When we are riding in a competition or in a school, following the classical-riding technique, we usually
ask him to bring his head down and curve his neck to achieve a beautiful
outline and for us to be able to control him more easily. However, if we
ask for his neck to become over-bent, we perhaps don't realise that we
are therefore blocking his forward vision so that he in essence cannot see
where he is going, a potentially dangerous state of affairs. It is therefore
essential that as we approach a jump or an obstacle, we let him have his
head not only so that he can lengthen his neck in preparation for the
jump, but so that he can clearly see what it is that he is jumping.

Distinguishing colour

You may also have noticed that your horse perhaps will shy at a red cone
yet stride past a blue one without so much as a glance. He may attack an
orange and white vertical jump with enthusiasm, yet will run out every
time at a green and white jump.

Until very recently, it was thought that horses, like many other
animals, saw the world entirely in black and white. However, studies
carried out by the Equine Research Foundation, among others, have
revealed that the horse does in fact see in colour, known as 'dichromatic
colour vision', rather than sharing the usual trichromatic colour vision
with humans. This means that he is able to see green, blue and yellow
but not red – similar to colour blindness in humans. To him, red has been
shown to simply appear as a shade of green.

This difference in the ability to distinguish colours is controlled
through filters, or 'cones' in the eyes. Humans with no colour blindness

typically have three cones which can pick up red, green, blue and yellow colour ranges whereas horses, on the whole, only have two cones (Figure 5); though of course, as with humans, there are always exceptions to the rule and some horses appear to be able to distinguish colours better than others.

A benefit that dichromats have over trichromats is the ability to discriminate colours in dim light. Although colours to a horse in daylight may not be as varied as those seen through the human eye, at dusk, twilight and at night the horse comes into his own. At night a horse can distinguish colour better than a human, this ability allows the horse to see the possibility of oncoming danger even at night.

Figure 5. Horses are not colour blind but most can't see red.
(illustrations by Jennifer Bell)

On the whole, my view is that dichromatic sight is as useful to the horse as trichromatic sight is to us humans. It rarely causes immense problems to horse and rider, indicating that a horse just views his world in varying shades of green. As a grazing animal, the horse's food is also in shades of green and he has no need, for example, to pick out the reds of ripe fruits as primates do. However, this limited ability to distinguish colour should be borne in mind when schooling or riding, particularly when jumping (Figures 6a and b). If the horse is unable to see a marked difference between a coloured rail and the ground below it, he is of course more likely to misjudge the height he needs in order to clear it; hence the reason why many jumps are painted in two contrasting colours.

fact

Research in Hungary discovered that, unlike horses, flies do see red: they are attracted to red cars – so don't paint your horsebox red!
The study also found that compared to the white horse, black horses attracted 25 times as many flies, and brown horses attracted 15 times as many.

Light intensity

Care must also be taken when changing the intensity of light quickly around a horse, who in general is much more sensitive to light than we are. Contrary to what you might think, a horse has excellent night vision yet will struggle slightly to see clearly in bright sunlight. For this reason, many horses become spooked when being asked to march smartly through the sunshine into a fairly dark trailer or stable. It becomes rather more understandable when you consider that he's unable to see clearly, is worried by the change of intensity of lighting and is confused about what you're asking him to do. His vision is temporarily impaired and in the horse's case, this can prove literally fatal. In these situations, simply try to remain calm, understand why he's wary about doing what you've asked, walk him very slowly into the stable or trailer and allow him time to stop and get his bearings. By allowing him to adjust his eyesight slowly to cope with the varying natural light will prevent problems occurring in the future.

**Figures 6a and b. a. The same jump as we would see it (top) and
b. as the horse would see it, where red is seen as a green (bottom)**

So now you understand the basic process of how your horse sees the world around him and how his perception of his surroundings can affect his emotions and behaviour, you should incorporate this understanding into *your* behaviour when you are working with and around him, to ensure he feels safe and at ease at all times.

Visual laterality

Intriguing results, released in 2008, following studies carried out by De Boyer Des Roches, Richard-Yris et al., 'Laterality and emotions: Visual laterality in the domestic horse', indicated that horses may view objects in either a neutral or negative light, reacting to both in a different way.

A number of mares were used in trials (also carried out on fishes, chicks and toads with similar results) and were subsequently introduced to three unfamiliar objects. When an object was perceived as non-threatening, the mares seemed to prefer to use their right eye to view it, whereas a potentially negative object was viewed through the left eye. The mares also principally used their right nostril to sniff the unfamiliar object, indicating that there are definitely areas of the brain which are consistently used to process new information.

These findings are relatively new to the equine world and could potentially mean a breakthrough in training techniques.

fact

When exploring a novel object, mares used their right eyes, while they showed a slight tendency to use their left eyes for negative objects.

So, working on the theory that the majority of horses (males as well as females) view objects in the same way, we can then assume that if a horse does not want to go past an object because he considers it to be threatening, he will focus on it through his left eye. This eye is attached to the right side of the brain which, as we've already discussed, is the 'instinctive' side, rather than the side which uses logic and reasoning. As a result, the horse is then likely to shy away, or jump to his right, away from the object.

fact

Horses who spend time in fields are often more familiar with unusual sights and sounds and have better balance when negotiating uneven ground than those horses who are mostly stabled.

Rationalising an unknown object

If we understand this left-eye-first way of looking at objects, then perhaps we can overcome the negativity by allowing the horse to see an object with his left eye, then turning him around and walking him back towards it again, so that he then sees it with his right eye, therefore being able to see it in a logical, more reasonable way. By taking him past it again and again on both sides, he may well be able to process the information and come to the natural conclusion that the object poses no threat at all. Once you sense he is happy and relaxed once more, try turning his left eye to the object and see if there is any response, to gauge how successful the exercise has been.

I have tried this approach with a few equine clients and in each instance, it has indeed worked. Although these studies are still in their infancy, I suspect that by using his right eye when passing a 'problem' object, the horse is able to transfer the information to the left side of his brain, reassuring himself that it isn't a problem at all. In humans, we know that, similarly, new information and new skills are passed to the right side of our brain more than the left side in the initial stages. However, once this knowledge has been processed sufficiently and has become familiar through practice, it is transferred over to the left half of our brain (Johnsgard, 1981). It appears therefore that the link between the right side of the brain and new, potentially unsettling, information is not restricted solely to humans but horses too.

In humans, research has shown that it is the right side of the brain which controls the way in which both our eyes are able to move together. It may be then, that it is also the right side which tells us that both of our eyes should work together in that specific way, complementing each other and giving us a more rounded picture of the world in which we live (de Renzi, 1988). The results of studies using animals that have eyes placed laterally, such as fishes, toads, chicks and horses, showed that they tend to use their left eyes in response to an oncoming predator. The fact that they use their left and right eyes completely independently of each other indicates that a different view of the world is given by each eye, rather than that rounded view achieved when both eyes are used in harmony. Chicks which used both eyes together, it was suggested, are able to perceive the world as dictated by the right side of their brain.

Interestingly, additional research ('The Master and his Emissary', Ian McGilchrist, 2009), revealed that human emotions principally stem from the right side of our brain, yet anger is controlled by the more logical left side, indicating that, in some way, the anger emotion can be more controlled than other emotions (despite the seeming lack of ability in some humans). Using the same theory then, it may well be that a horse seeing a potential source of danger or negativity in his left eye first, would be more likely to avoid that source at all costs, listening to the right 'fight or flight' side of his brain. An angered response, stemming from the left side of his brain would most probably be a learned response rather than an instinct, and would certainly come into play as a last resort.

Most of us, usually whilst out hacking, will have experienced the situation where our horse will spot an object he instantly takes exception to – a blue wheelie bin for example. He will see the object with his left eye first and, his illogical thoughts telling him that it could hurt him, inevitably shies away. Despite his anxiety and irrational behaviour, you may manage to push him on and he will likely comply but dance and jog past the bin. Not a pleasant experience for either of you. After a few minutes, the anxiety will have left both of you and you will either have forgotten the incident or be confident that now he's seen the object he'll realise it isn't dangerous and remember that on the way back. However, on the return journey home, he spots the same wheelie bin and yet again shies away. 'What an idiot!' you'll no doubt have thought. However, there is a very good reason why your horse reacts in this way and as always, it has a very strong link to the way in which he sees the world around him, a view which is very different from ours.

On the first occasion, perhaps the wheelie bin was placed outside on the street, against a wall. To put yourself in your horse's hooves, imagine that scene with the bin against the wall as a framed picture. As he looks at the picture in front of him he will see a row of houses with a bin outside the first house and a line of trees on the other side of the road. This is something he hasn't seen before, he doesn't recognise it and so his mind is shrieking for him to avoid it all costs. He is therefore wary of the object and so tries to move away from it. A reassuring nudge from you however, often convinces him that he can rush past it without fear of it running after him. On his return however, he now sees everything in reverse order and so to him it's a different picture. This time the first house is now the last one and instead of a row of houses he sees countryside after the house and a row of houses behind him. The horse is seeing a completely different wheelie bin in a different environment which, to his mind, he needs to be cautious of and so may shy again.

He is unable to rationalise that the blue wheelie bin he saw earlier is in fact exactly the same wheelie bin he's seeing again albeit from a different angle. This is a whole new kettle of fish for him and so naturally, he is acting on his instinct and moving away from this new strange object. He isn't being awkward or naughty; he's simply reacting to situations which make him uneasy.

I often think that this aspect of a horse's thinking should be considered when competing in jumping competitions. As the horse goes over a jump he sees it from one view and if he goes over the jump the other way it has a different view to the horse, and therefore it is not the same jump. Pre-competition, we riders walk the course so that we become familiar with the types of jumps involved, the number of strides needed to clear each one and perhaps so that we can identify where we can take out a stride or two in order to achieve a good time. However, this is for riders' benefit only. Shouldn't the horse be acquainted with the course too? It would seem sensible and considerate to also allow the horse a walk around the course, viewing the jumps from all sides, before the bell rings for our round to begin. In doing so, we may well find that he is more confident, less thrown by any of the jumps and overall performs much better.

tip

So you have walked the course – but what about the horse! Allow your horse to see all sides of the arena before you jump. Horses see things differently to us; approaching a jump one way is one picture/view to the horse. Approach the same jump from the other way and for the horse it is a different picture/view.

Iridology

It is often said that the eyes are 'the windows to the soul' and although this is a fanciful phrase, the science of iridology, the study of the iris, has lent a certain amount of credence to it. We talk about how a horse has a 'kind' eye or 'angry' eye and we also know that bright, shining eyes are visible signs of good health, whereas dull, listless eyes indicate potential illness or depression. It is exactly the same with humans of course. Someone who is healthy, eats and sleeps well and enjoys exercise is likely to have bright, sparkling eyes, whereas someone who is in ill health, or someone who is a substance abuser, can have what we commonly refer to as 'dead' eyes: there is no life, light or personality within them.

Iridology has been studied for thousands of years, with significant progress made in this field by physician Dr Ignatz von Peczeley in 1881.

As a boy, Dr von Peczeley caught an owl and in doing so, accidentally broke its leg. Obviously horrified, he stared at the owl's face and as he did so, he noticed a black mark appearing in one of its eyes. Taking it home and nursing it back to health, he noticed that over time, as the leg healed, the mark in the owl's eye changed colour, until it faded to a small white mark with several dots surrounding it. This incident led Dr von Peczeley to conduct studies in iridology in later life, the results of which are still being used in further research today.

During the Second World War, Syd Mercer worked in the cavalry on the south coast of England, during which time he obviously saw a good number of injured, dying and dead horses. Having a specific interest in equines, he began to examine their eyes in various stages of health and subsequently, he too noticed the connection between the animals' irises and their state of health, going on to essentially introduce and develop the whole topic of equine iridology to both medical and public society, later using his knowledge, research and experience to help several horses go on and win a number of high profile races.

Studies into equine iridology continue to this day, led by American veterinarian Dena Eckerdt and human iridologist Mercedes Colburn.

Body language

Body language is extremely important to horses, particularly herds in the wild, and they are very sensitive to the slightest change in posture or behaviour (Goodwin, 1999). Generally, if the dominant stallion in a herd suddenly raises his head and stands absolutely still, this is the signal for the rest of the herd to be alarmed and on alert. As they are grazing and going about their daily business, you will notice that they keep half an eye on their leader, constantly checking his body language for signs of tension. This consistent state of alertness is vital for the survival of the herd.

Similarly, a rounded, puffed out, body and high head carriage indicates excitement or arousal, whilst when the head is relaxed and carried midway you will observe that the body is usually flattish through the back with the body and limbs also relaxed. Every part of a horse's body can display exactly what he is feeling and communicate this effectively. It is simply up to us to learn to understand him.

A psychic ability?

I shut my eyes in order to see. – PAUL GAUGIN

Moving away from the practical and scientific to the metaphysical for a moment, psychic ability in animals has been tested and documented over many decades, with countless stories told about how an animal has somehow been able to 'foretell' an accident and has saved its owner as a result. Although this type of theory is invariably difficult to prove, it is widely accepted that animals of all species can in some way sense when a natural disaster is likely to occur. Even if you haven't seen this happening in the wild in real life, films based around a natural disaster will invariably include a scene whereby a flock of birds or a host of forest animals flee the area before a tidal wave hits or a fire wipes out acres of woodland. Even domestic animals have been known to behave strangely before an earthquake or tornado hits with birds becoming restless and fluttering around in their cages, and dogs howling.

As fanciful as this may seem, think for a moment about a less dramatic natural incident, perhaps when a harmless storm was brewing. Did any of your horses or other pets behave in a way which was unusual? Keep a close eye on them the next time this happens to see if they are trying to communicate with you.

Rather than just forming the basis of a good old spooky story however, scientific research has shown that many animals are indeed, in many instances although not all, able to pick up on subtle changes in the earth and atmosphere, which many humans are oblivious to. But not all of us!

In his studies, ('The Conscious Universe', 1997 and 'Entangled Minds', 2006), Dean Radin carried out a number of tests to uncover whether any humans also had the gift of foresight. Volunteers were wired to monitors that measured any change in skin conduction, heart rate and blood pressure, before being shown a number of photos designed to elicit calm, arousal or distress emotions.

Amazingly, the monitors showed actual physical changes, which would be expected in a human for the nature of the photograph about to be shown, taking place before the photos were even shown to the volunteers, demonstrating that their bodies were anticipating their future emotions and reacting accordingly. These responses were recorded as being highest before being shown an image which was either disturbing or arousing. Could this perhaps indicate a deep-seated instinct, present yet unrecognised in humans, specifically to protect us against danger or a more positive anticipation of a sexual union?

Dr Rollin McCraty carried out similar tests, but this time also included the monitoring of other changes to brain and heart activity. Again, both organs were able to 'anticipate' the future emotions and react accordingly. As a means of testing out the phrase 'gut instinct', changes in the intestines were also recorded and it was shown that the intestines reacted in exactly the same way.

All this simply goes to show that there is indeed a direct effect between our emotions and the reactions given by the rest of our body. It also shows that our body can react without our even being aware that we are feeling specific emotions to any great degree.

Transferring this theory to horses, a groom for one of my clients (who could, I think it would be fair to say, be a little 'difficult' at times), noticed that each time the lady came to look at her horse, the animal would begin to work up a sweat before he even saw her. Like the experiments carried out on humans to see if they could anticipate emotions before the trigger was even given, it was as if the horse was somehow able to anticipate her imminent arrival and became extremely anxious at the thought of it.

Another rider reported how she was puzzled when her horse, during a normal, calm jumping lesson, shot off to the other side of the field and refused to budge, despite the shouting, digging heels and threat of the whip. This rider, like so many of us, was under the mistaken impression that her horse was being awkward for the sake of it and, being shaken after nearly falling off, was set to punish him. However, several minutes later, a great crack was heard, and one of the branches fell off a large tree which was hanging over one of the jumps. If the horse hadn't acted appropriately in the way he did, there was a fair chance that both horse and rider would have been injured. Needless to say, there were many apologies, pats and treats given afterwards!

My own view is that there is little psychic ability, in the sense of paranormal (i.e. outside the possibilities defined by natural laws), behind the way in which a horse (or a human for that matter) behaves. Although the horse could be considered to be limited in his visual capabilities he, like many other animals, has managed to retain the natural instincts he has always needed to survive in the wild – the ability to sense a potential predator at a distance, to seek out a potential mate and to avoid a potentially dangerous situation before it arises.

Remember the phrase 'I can't believe my eyes'? Although we humans have grown lazy over the last few thousand years or so by relying heavily on our eyesight more than any other sense in order to identify and process information, a horse has been designed to question what he sees, relying on his sense of smell and hearing to support the information transmitted by his eyes. He therefore has the basic instinct and natural ability to support any shortcomings in his other senses.

a.

b.

These three horses have their attention focussed forward and are coordinating sight, smell and hearing to assess the surroundings:

a. A three-day-eventer at an international show waiting for his turn to compete.

b. In more relaxed surroundings, but this horse is also using all his senses to distinguish friend or foe. Behind stands a masked horse!

c. Keeping a watchful eye.

c.

This horse shows he has no need to be particularly watchful; there is a softness in his eyes that says he shows no fear of who may be approaching.

I hope that in this chapter, I have been able to shed some light on your horse's behaviour which, in the past, may have been puzzling (and no doubt frustrating) to you. By understanding the way in which he looks at his surroundings, this should also help with both your relationship and your riding performance as a team. Punishing him for not complying with your instructions despite not understanding the reason why is neither effective nor constructive, and this lack of communication between you can only lead to mistrust, dislike and a thoroughly miserable relationship for both of you.

chapter six

SMELL: THE HORSE'S SIXTH SENSE?

There is more to the sense of smell than meets the eye!

Like most mammals, horses rely heavily on their sense of smell – the olfactory sense – not only in order to survive but to socialise and to reproduce.

The horse has an extremely effective nasal function which not only supports his other senses but, it could be argued, is possibly his most important sense when it comes to providing a link with emotions.

We have already discussed the fact that, although the horse has a superb visual ability which allows him to see movement far into the distance, his blind spots and relative lack of ability to see details of stationary objects far away means his sight is not perfect. However, a horse's nose will rarely fail him, allowing him to pick up on the most subtle of scents which humans are rarely able to do.

This extraordinary sense of smell is the key to the horse's basic need to recognise not only other horses, but the emotions being felt and emitted by individual humans and other animals around him.

When two horses who are strangers meet, they will invariably get close to each other, face to face and almost touch noses by way of an introduction. You will see that they will snort very loudly and sniff each other, often tossing their heads. By doing this, they are of course smelling each other and using scent as a way of summing each other up very quickly (McGreevey, 2004). The information they are receiving may be telling them whether the other horse is in season or perhaps whether it is aggressive or sociable. In fact it is not yet known whether or not an initial introduction such as this indicates that a future meeting will subsequently mean that the two horses will then be able to identify and remember each other from their scent alone.

In can be argued, as stated in Chapter 5, that humans are lazy when it comes to utilising all their senses fully; relying heavily on the sense of sight to identify objects and other people in order to make a judgement and process any necessary information. This has its limitations, however.

Have you ever looked at a person who perhaps dresses or acts very differently from the 'norm' and instantly decided that you don't like them

A horse will use his sense of smell to recognise a danger or a threat from another horse.

because they are so different, or even perhaps conclude that they pose a threat to you in some way? You may be surprised to learn later then, that they are a professional carer of some sort or have carried out a heroic deed.

Adversely, I'm sure you'll agree that there a large number of people in the world who, although outwardly seem very down to earth and respectable, hide several undesirable traits and can even be potentially very dangerous.

Although this should obviously tell us that our eyes really can't be trusted on their own on many occasions, we either do not bring, or are not capable of bringing, our other senses into play, so that we can better trust our own judgement.

Many animals however – animals who have retained their ingrained instinct to recognise danger and potential mates – are equipped with a superb set of senses which they often use in harmony with each other to accurately summarise a particular individual or situation.

Think of a time when you felt afraid or wary of something, particularly if you were alone and in the dark. Your sight will of course have been limited due to the lack of available light – or perhaps you will have been unable to see anything at all, so you will have instinctively strained your ears to see if you could hear anything, or perhaps you may have felt your way along the surface of a wall if the terrain was unsafe. If you'd also been able to use your sense of smell as another extremely valuable tool in assessing your surroundings, it may have been able to play a large part in reassuring you that you were safe, or could have alerted you if someone else was approaching.

I think that humans tend to look upon smell as being the sense which is needed least. In most instances, this may well be the case. Those who lose their sense of feeling often face danger as they are unable to tell if an object is hot and can burn themselves. Similarly, we often feel particular sympathy for those who have lost their eyesight or their hearing completely; although as we (and animals for that matter) age, these senses often tend to weaken and become increasingly ineffective. However, for a horse, particularly one who lives among a wild herd, the sense of smell could be considered to be of fundamental importance. Using smell, it can identify a potential mate who is prime for mating and reproduction, as well as sense danger from a considerable distance. These abilities are something which his eyes would not necessarily be capable of – and neither would ours. Perhaps if we were to learn how to develop our sense of smell more acutely so it acts effectively for us, it would prove to be of immense benefit, taking over when our other senses begin to fail us, as it is also evident that as one sense begins to fail, the others seem to strengthen, allowing us to continue functioning effectively.

It is worth noting here that even as we grow older and our sight or our hearing (or both) begin to weaken, our sense of smell usually remains strong and consistent – proving that it is not such a minor sense after all and could be used much more effectively, as a horse uses his.

Although we unfortunately don't have the same sensitivity as animals and their ability to smell subtle changes in the atmosphere, potential predators or friends in the distance and fear in others, our nose can still transmit powerful messages to the rest of our body. The smell of fresh fish and chips cooking for example can trigger immediate hunger pangs; a familiar scent of perfume can remind us of a female family member or friend who is no longer with us, which makes us feel sad, and the sudden waft of 'seaside' on a car journey can tell us that we're nearing the coast. This connection between smell, emotions and memory is a powerful one, and is one which also resides in the horse.

In Chapter 5 you may remember, I discussed how most horses will initially approach and smell an object with the right nostril first. The information gained from this first sniff: 'What is it? Is it pleasant or unpleasant? Is it likely to harm me? Is this a familiar smell?' is then transmitted to the left side of his brain, the area which stores past experiences. This then, would seemingly indicate that not only are horses learning from the smells but also that those smells are directly associated with past experiences. Not only that, but all smells and odours are committed to memory and may trigger relevant emotions attached to how the horse felt during that particular experience.

fact

Horses, but in particular young horses, use their right nostrils first to smell a new object to gain an understanding of it.

tip

Allow your horse to sniff anything that is new so that he can explore the object in his own way, and then register that it is safe and secure.

fact

In an experiment it was found that humans who sniffed through their left nostril (which connects to their left brain) showed slightly better skills at identifying odours by name. When they sniffed through their right nostril they found the odours more pleasant.

tip

Watch which nostril your horse uses when sniffing, it may be a key to his experience at that moment.

Can you think back to your childhood and remember any smells which you remember made you feel a certain way? Perhaps the smell of the beach during your summer holidays, the chlorine from your local swimming pool or the gingerbread your mum used to bake. Do they make you feel sad, comforted, wistful or anxious?

This is important information when dealing with a horse who is nervous in a particular situation or with a particular person. Over time it may be possible for him, given positive reinforcement in the form of food treats or other such reward, to associate a certain smell (the smell of the horsebox, the farrier or the vet for example) not with an unpleasant experience, but with the reward which will inevitably follow it. You won't see an immediate change in behaviour, but with perseverance and persistence, you should slowly begin to see his attitude changing for the better when under stress.

If you spend time watching your horse grazing happily in a field, you will, like most horse owners, probably remember a time when your horse's head suddenly shot up for no apparent reason. He would have been focusing on something in the distance, his ears forward and twitching, his nostrils flaring. It is likely that at that precise moment you had no idea what had disturbed him, but it is guaranteed his senses picked up something in the distance that interested him in some way. By focusing all his attention and his sight, smell and hearing, he was in fact trying to decipher exactly what it was in the distance that had disturbed his contented grazing.

In many instances, a few minutes later something, or someone, familiar would have come into view. If this had been an equine or human friend, the sighting might have been accompanied by much whinnying and excitement. Although you were unable to rely upon your senses to give you this information so far in advance, your horse's refined faculties ensured this result. In the wild this ability is of course invaluable for the horse.

This heightened awareness is rarely switched off, even when the animal is asleep. Having his senses in play at all times, far from being annoying to the horse has, over thousands of years, proved vital not only for his survival but during everyday life and for reproduction too.

Smelling the ground will identify if it's safe to lie down; the horse can check to establish if a predator has passed by.

In studies carried out on humans by Finkelmeyer, Kellermann et al. ('Effects of aversive odour presentation on inhibitory control in the Stroop colour-word interference task', 2010), it was proven that smell can directly affect emotions in animals and therefore also affect their behaviour. For example, we do know that a horse will shy away from a bad smell and, similarly, perfume on a woman can excite a stallion. Not only that, but various emotional states were also shown to affect specific functions carried out by the brain, including memory. Unlike vision and hearing, smell and emotion are centred in the same area of the brain and the results from several studies have taught us that in horses, smell can trigger an emotional response such as fear or sexual arousal. From this research, I would therefore suggest that of all his senses, smell and emotion have the strongest link in a horse.

Flehmen

When something catches your horse's attention, either when at rest or when you are out riding, you will often note that he raises his head, stretches out his neck and pulls his upper lip upwards before curling it back, exposing the gums and the incisor teeth, looking for all the world like he's laughing.

Although this posture this looks very comical, what is truly happening is that he is inhaling the air. In order to test the air he will in fact stop breathing for a moment to process the smell before taking another breath to clarify his findings. This practice is known as 'flehmen' and is common to many animals.

Studies have shown that flehmen, although carried out to a certain extent in most horses and foals of both sexes, has been shown to be a prominent activity among males, particularly stallions who are trying to detect if any mare nearby is in season.

After giving birth, mares tend to show an increase in flehmen activity. They will sniff their newborn foal and his surrounding membranes to commit his scent to memory, then display an unusually high amount of flehmen over the next few hours. It is not yet certain why this should be so, other than it might be a way of being able to identify her own foal in the future, although it could possibly be a primitive form of a medical check-up.

Urine and faeces also seem to trigger the horse's nose, with many compelled to sniff the grass where another horse has recently urinated. This is particularly the case with stallions identifying the urine and faeces of mares, indicating that this too has a reproductive reason.

This horse is following the scent of another horse by identifying the urine and faeces trails.

Although there is as yet no scientific research to support the theory, it is felt to be particularly important that young, orphaned colts are exposed to deposits of mare's urine and that flehmen is encouraged, to nurture their normal sexual development.

The vomeronasal organ

Most mammals are known to emit body chemicals through their skin and into the air, particularly when feeling a particular emotion and the horse will pull specific particles of chemicals (particularly the scent-based hormones known as pheromones) in the air through his mouth and into the vomeronasal organ or VNO. Not a great deal is yet known about this organ but, in horses, it is believed that it is connected to the nose and has a significant effect on his behaviour.

Flehmen gives a horse the ability to not only identify individuals, but also to sense the emotions of a human or animal in his personal space. Once the air is drawn in, the horse will process the information in his VNO and pass it on to what are called the olfactory or vomeronasal bulbs in his brain.

right It looks like this horse is laughing at something but maybe he has picked up something in the air.

left Horses have the ability to smell subtle changes in the atmosphere whether it is from potential predators or friends.

According to Sharon L. Crowell-Davis's article on flehmen in 'Compendium Equine', 2008, this activity is thought to be instinctive, not learned.

In animals including cats, cows, dogs, goats and pigs as well as horses, Jacobson (1813) noted that the VNO is located in the front part of the nose, but is very much concealed. It consists of cells which are able to receive smells, those which perform secretions. The VMO is then connected to the olfactory bulb, or gland, in the brain by a series of nerves.

The theme of the VNO and its role in reproduction was the focus of experiments carried out on guinea pigs by Planel (1953). The results of these experiments showed that when the VNO was impaired in some way, many males failed to perform and for those couples which were able to copulate, females seldom became pregnant.

Powers and Winans (1975) found that these results were consistent in hamsters, too. However, they went one step further in determining that if the VNO was damaged or removed when the animal was young and sexually underdeveloped, then the results were magnified. However, if the animal had successfully performed with one or other mates in the past, before the damage or removal had occurred, the results were less pronounced.

Further investigation uncovered the possible chain of events that occurs in the VNO, which in turn triggers sexual stimulation. It is thought that when the organ is stimulated, it releases a specific hormone, which in turn increases the level of another specific, separate hormone whose sole objective is to encourage sexual performance (Clancy et al., 1988; Coquelin et al., 1984; Meredith and Fernandez-Fewell, 1994).

It is not simply the case however, that once sexually stimulated, the animal considers any potential mate (i.e. any mare or stallion) fair game. A connection to an appropriate mate will be made through the inhalation of pheromones and an animal will in fact be able to identify who it should mate with – a process which takes place in the olfactory bulb (Kaba et al., 1994) (Figure 7). For females, a subsequent connection with a male other than their original mate will usually result in non-fertilisation.

Studies carried out by S. Nimmermark ('Odour Influence on Wellbeing and Health with Specific Focus on Animal Production Emissions', 2004), revealed that 'stimulation of the olfactory system induces approach

Human brain   Equine brain

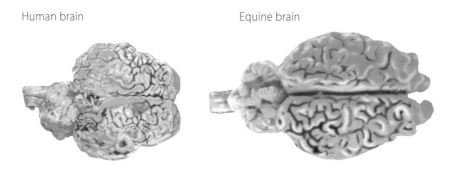

Figure 7. Human and equine brains.
The olfactory gland of a horse (pink area) is much larger than that of the human.

or avoidance behaviour' and that smells related to food can in fact often govern the horse's taste: if a horse tastes something that made him ill he remembers the smell, which in turn stops him from eating that food again. A smell can also, he says, act as a warning to both humans and animals. This fact is well supported in the animal kingdom, with skunks and toads in particular equipped with the ability to spray a dreadful-smelling scent, something which is instinctively known by all potential predators who, on the whole, give them a wide berth.

Nimmermark's findings indicate then that the scent we give off as humans can in fact tell the horse whether he should approach us or turn tail (approach or avoidance). He will immediately be able to sense whether someone has an angry, aggressive personality and will instinctively use avoidance tactics; whereas, for example, a young child with no fear may well intrigue him and encourage him to socialise (particularly if he should also sense that a treat is in store!)

Studies investigating whether or not this organ exists in similar form and function in humans are still ongoing. What is both apparent and interesting, however, is that the horse has a prominent vomeronasal organ, an accessory olfactory structure, which is nearly vestigial in humans. This gives rise to the question whether or not we have this same ability to identify other individuals through smell alone but have lost the instinct to use it (Johnson et al., 1985). It also suggests that the sense of smell is less fundamental for survival and reproduction in humans as it is in other animals, including the horse.

According to Jason Bernstein in his 1999 paper, 'Sixth Sense: The Vomeronasal Organ', scientist David Berliner was studying human skin composition in the 1960s using leftover skin cells from the inside of used plaster casts. Over time, he discovered that when he left opened vials of skin deposits around the laboratory, the atmosphere among his assistants became warmer and friendlier. Adversely, after a few months when the vials were sealed, this behaviour, he noted, was considerably reduced. This led him to question the existence of 'odourless' human pheromones and whether our VNO acts as some sort of 'sixth sense', or a heightened sense of unconscious smell.

To many, these suggestions are extremely far fetched and although I think there may be at least some truth to the theory, I would in fact further question whether the skin cells were indeed odourless or whether their scent was simply too subtle for humans to pick up. After all, when a cat rubs itself against table legs, fence posts or indeed its owner's legs, all other cats in the vicinity can immediately identify that scent, yet we cannot. It is as if invisible to our sense of smell.

Horses and dogs in particular have a much larger olfactory bulb than humans, suggesting that their sense of smell plays a much larger part in their sensory and emotional systems, particularly when interpreting the world around them.

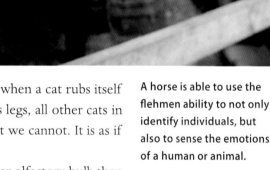

A horse is able to use the flehmen ability to not only identify individuals, but also to sense the emotions of a human or animal.

fact

The olfactory structures (smell glands) of primates, and especially humans, have greatly diminished and, in relation to humans, horses have an extremely large olfactory bulb giving them the ability to smell things that humans cannot pick up.

fact

In humans and horses, olfactory and emotional systems are distinctively different but, in both species, there are reasons to suspect that these systems influence each other on the social level. If horses have a larger olfactory capability than humans, it can be assumed that smell plays a very important part in equine emotional reactions.

Bernstein, in his research, also reflected upon the fact that male mice are able to produce chemosignals which automatically trigger an early puberty in immature females. This led me to wonder if, among species that are presented with difficult circumstances in which to try and ensure survival, or perhaps a herd of horses whose numbers are on the decline, whether the males would naturally begin to trigger puberty among fillies, encouraging reproduction at a time when the survival of the herd – or indeed the species – was in question.

Sensing emotions through scent

Nerves and tension

But what has all this to do with your interaction with your horse? Suggestions have been made that the horse, in addition to picking up on any tension you may be experiencing, can also receive information about you through the secretion of your own pheromones, which could explain why he will lower his nose and sniff you as you stand next to him. He may not be simply looking for titbits, but discovering how confident you are, ascertaining your mood and picking up on any anxiety (Lansade et al., 2008). Whether a human is fearful, angry or calm, the horse can pick up the individual chemical given off by the body through his VNO system. For this reason, whether you are fearful or nervous at a competition, and regardless of how confident you think your riding is, or even when arriving at the yard to prepare on the morning of a competition, your horse will be able to sense this and in turn become unnerved, often ultimately performing less well than usual.

Unfortunately, although you may be confident and looking forward to competing, some horses may be more sensitive than others and pick up on the nerves of the other horses and riders around him.

It is believed that the vomeronasal organ, or VNO, is connected to the nose and has a significant effect on a horse's behaviour.

Preparing a nervous horse for a competition

If you think that you, the horse or both of you are likely to be nervous at a competition, prepare beforehand, beginning with yourself. On the morning of the event, or even on the drive to the yard, carry out some deep breathing exercises to slow down your heart rate and increase the oxygen being transmitted to your brain and lungs. Next, visualise the pair of you completing the perfect round in absolute harmony. Focus on an image of you finishing the round feeling jubilant and proud. Convince yourself that you'll finish in one piece, that your horse will perform beautifully and that you'll both return to the yard feeling delighted. In this way, your horse will be met not by a rider quaking in their boots (which doesn't exactly instil confidence) but by someone he knows and hopefully trusts, who is confident and happy which, in turn, will make him feel safe and secure. In this state, you should also take the time to give him some personal attention to ensure he remains in the right frame of mind. A massage would be a wonderful way to start the day, loosening up his muscles, ensuring he feels comfortable and helping the bonding process. Although you can't prevent others from giving off fearful chemicals during the day, you're giving your horse the best chance of being able to take the scents on board and not be so strongly affected by them.

The influence of odours

The ability to sense the emotions of others through scent, it has been suggested, is also present in humans. In experiments conducted by Ackerl et al., 2002, a number of women were able to distinguish between fearful and non-fearful humans, through scent alone. However, on a day-to-day basis, this ability is either reduced or is simply not used.

Although essential oils and homeopathic remedies have become popular again in recent years, they have of course been used to cure conditions and ailments for centuries. This would indicate that we humans do at least have some understanding of how smell can affect us physically and emotionally. In research based on this theory, it was discovered, for example, that although lavender is considered to be the principal oil for calming emotions and inducing sleep, it was lemon balm which in fact had the best calming effects. With this in mind, although essential oils should not be applied directly to the horse's skin, you might like to try applying a few drops to his rug or to some wood in his stall to try to induce a calming effect but check to see if the horse likes the smell of the oil before applying it.

Odours which horses consider to be unpleasant (which we would naturally assume to be smells connected with artificial products and chemicals) have been shown to induce stress and ill-temper in the animals. Consider, for example, if you were sitting on an aeroplane for nine hours, next to someone who was wearing a particularly pungent and offensive perfume. No doubt after a period of nose wrinkling and sneezing, you'd begin to develop a headache and would feel particularly out of sorts and irritated. Now consider how the horse feels if he is made to live permanently next to a similarly offensive smell, with no means of escaping from it. You might not be able to recognise that the smell is offensive – but then the person wearing the perfume on the aeroplane didn't either!

Take the time to make a tour of your horse's surroundings. Are there any compost heaps, pots of paint, tins of hoof polish or similar strong-smelling products housed next to him? If so, rehouse them, or him, elsewhere if you can. Unfortunately, some equine-focused products have also been shown to cause tension in horses through awful odours. The best way to tell is simply to allow him to sniff any potential culprits in his immediate surroundings and judge his resulting behaviour. If he's interested and happy to investigate it, then chances are it is fine where it is. If he puts his ears back and turns his head away, you need to remove the offensive object.

One of the worst culprits for causing stress to a horse through smell in my view is the chemicals used on agricultural land. Some foul-smelling artificial fertilisers and pest control sprays can be smelled by humans miles away, so we can only wonder what it must be like for the horse whose home is in the very next field, whose smell glands are much more sensitive than ours and who is forced to smell that awful odour for days at a time, unable to block it out. If your turned-out horse shows signs of irritability at certain times, it may be that this is the reason. In which case, you could try moving him to a different field if possible until the smell dies down.

You can't lie to your horse

We as riders and horse owners tend to rely on our voice when communicating with our horses in the same way as we do with other humans, expecting it to have the same effect. However, according to Saslow, 2002, the tone and pitch of our voice can vary considerably, depending on our state of mind and emotions, making this 'tool' extremely inconsistent and questionable as an effective aid. Do you find that you're able to calm your horse using your voice as a tool?

If olfactory communication is indeed present but is not able to be used by humans when dealing with horses, this then means that we simply cannot lie to the animal. We can adjust our tone of voice and our stance (which are principal aids in riding) but, it is safe to say, we are unable to control the processes within our body.

Consider those undertaking a lie-detector test. Results are based on subtle changes which take place within the subject's body during the process, including blood pressure, heart rate, respiratory rate and the level of electricity transmitted by the skin. Although voice, expression and body positioning are the principal, outward signs of how a person is feeling, these can to some extent be controlled and so cannot be completely relied upon. For this reason, subconscious reactions are also measured in lie-detector tests.

This theory could then also be applied to how a horse can identify and interpret us when we're not aware of it. Even if you're feeling particularly anxious about something, however unrelated, he may be able to recognise this feeling through his sense of smell and perform badly as a result, even though you're confident that you've deliberately hidden it from him.

Prepare yourself before working with your horse

If you feel that despite giving verbal and physical reassurances to your horse you could be transmitting any anxieties, anger or negativity to him via his sense of smell, or any of his senses, you could be impairing your performance as a team and it may be that you need to work harder on yourself before you meet him. Meditation, physical exercise,

We often say: 'I can't believe my eyes' but a horse's strength is not in seeing but smell: 'I can't believe the smell'!

yoga and deep breathing exercises could all prove valuable in preparing yourself before heading off for a schooling or training session, resulting in improved performance from both you and the horse.

The connection between what a horse smells and the way in which it affects his emotions must become an integral part of our learning process, so that we too can begin to instinctively recognise which smells he adores and detests and how they affect his behaviour.

chapter seven

WHAT HORSES CAN HEAR AND HOW SOUNDS AFFECT THEIR EMOTIONS

The purpose of this book is not simply to give you a biological account of how each of a horse's senses works but how his emotions are inextricably linked to these senses. With hearing, this connection might not be obvious at the outset. However, by gaining an understanding of the physiology of his ears, the way they work and how this applies to his life in the wild, this information should be able to help you understand more about his reactions, and how your own reaction to them can indeed affect his emotions and therefore his behaviour.

As discussed in Chapter 5, the horse can be considered to have a limited visual ability. However, in the wild he must be alert at all times to the stealthy approach of a potential predator and so he uses all his senses in harmony, constantly scanning the environment for signs of danger. His sensitive nose will be able to pick up the scent of any unfamiliar animal from an impressive distance and his ears are always swivelling like small radars, designed specifically to pick up the slightest noise such as the snap of a twig or rustling leaves which could signify a threat.

It is this incredibly effective early-warning system that has helped the wild horse to survive for thousands of years.

His ears are always swivelling like small radars, designed specifically to pick up the slightest noise.

Exceptional hearing

The horse's sense of hearing is exceptional. Although he is often unable to pick up sounds transmitted at a very low frequency, which we can perhaps hear, he *is* able to recognise sounds transmitted at a particularly high frequency, similar in fact to dogs. Studies carried out by Heffner (1998) and Heffner and Heffner (1983, 1984 and 1986) have shown that a horse can actually hear sounds in excess of 33,000Hz, whereas a human's natural range is limited to under 20,000Hz (Figure 8).

Horses are able to recognise sounds transmitted at a particularly high frequency.

fact

Horses rely more on hearing than on sight. They have the ability of localising sound and higher frequencies than humans, such as a twig snapping in the distance, which may trigger a horse's reflex defences.

tip

If you notice alertness or anxiety in your horse, try and reassure him with a measured voice, not with tension or a higher pitch.

fact

Horses recognise the voices of their social partners even when they can't see them, and that explains their reactions when they are separated.

It is not so much the range of the pitch which is impressive in a horse however, but his ability to identify the slightest of sounds which would go undetected by most of us.

This difference in hearing ability should be considered when planning where a horse is to be housed. For example, horses stabled on farms have been shown to be significantly disturbed and unsettled by the ultrasonic sounds given off by rodent repellents, which are often used in such an environment.

So what makes him able to hear so well? The horse can move his outer ears (known as pinnae) 180 degrees by way of the ten muscles in each ear, compared to the human's paltry three. In this way, he can listen to sounds occurring in front of him, to the side and behind him. This flexibility in physical structure assists him when trying to locate the general source of a sound. The cup shape of his ears means that he can capture the sound wave more effectively than our ears ever could, thus ensuring that he can hear noises which are completely out of our range.

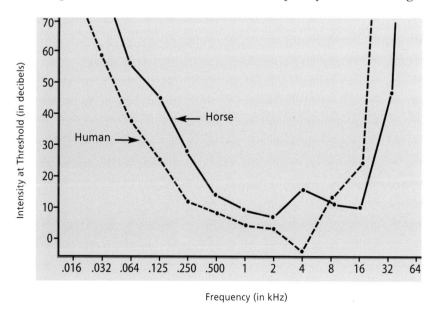

Figure 8. Comparison of equine and human hearing ranges
(graph redrawn by Carole Vincer)

above **You can see that these horses are swivelling their ears and listening whilst they are eating.**

above right **The cup shape of the horse's ears means that he can capture the sound wave more effectively than we humans.**

The sound waves will travel along his ear canal to his middle ear, where his eardrum will vibrate. These vibrations are then gradually passed along a multitude of small bones into his inner ear where the auditory nerve is found. This nerve then finally passes the message to his brain that there is a sound occurring and he needs to take notice. All this, of course, happens in a matter of seconds.

Like a human, the horse has what is known as 'binaural hearing', which means both ears will hear a sound simultaneously, although one ear will capture a noise a fraction of a second faster than the other one, advising him of the direction of the source of the sound.

The hearing sense is used to hear a sound, determine which direction it's coming from, and to provide information that the horse can use to recognise both the sound and the source itself.

The horse is programmed not to worry too much about finding out the exact source or nature of the noise however. In the wild, the few seconds it would take for him to play detective and process all the facts could literally mean the difference between life and death. So, once he has determined which direction a sound is emanating from, a more sensitive horse will immediately turn tail and run in the opposite direction, only stopping to think more about it once he's well clear of the situation.

In a domestic environment, a horse will often feel much safer and under less pressure to react. If he feels that he has the time and is safe enough to be interested in identifying the source, he will:

1. Stop grazing

2. Swivel his ears in the direction of the noise

3. Focus his eyes in that direction

4. Turn his whole head to look

5. Still his body

6. Turn and run if he's worried about what he hears.

Your horse will be able to hear someone or something approaching, often long before you will. He will attempt to bring all his senses into play at once, to identify what it is that has caught his attention, trying to catch sight of and focus on the distant object, flaring his nostrils in an attempt to identify it through flehmen and flicking his ears forward to gain more insight into the location of the noise.

Your horse will be able to hear someone or something approaching, often long before you will.

Hearing and nervousness

Whilst out riding, you may well have become frustrated when your horse spooked for no apparent reason. In this case, it may not be something he has seen which is unfamiliar and therefore considered to be potentially threatening, but it could well have been a noise which was out of the range of your hearing, which he could not identify or locate. As a rider, you can in actual fact, help to prevent your horse from spooking by tuning into his physical reactions and reassuring him before he has time to process the information. If you see something which you think may cause a nervous reaction, check the ear nearest to it. Has it flicked towards the

The human is wondering what the horse is hearing.

object? If so, he's seen it and he's considering what to do. If you can, try to distract him by talking calmly to him, offering him a treat or taking a slight diversion.

An older, more experienced or perhaps just a calmer horse is less likely to be spooked when out and about, whereas a more highly strung horse may be difficult to ride out, spooking and bolting at everything. It is worth considering, therefore, that your sensitive horse may have the characteristics of a herd leader. In the wild, the male will typically be the leader of the herd, and it is his job to be constantly on the alert, scanning his surroundings for signs of any potential threat to his mares. With this in mind, you may find that a male, particularly if he is territorial, will be more highly strung and likely to bolt.

With his aforementioned exceptional hearing, unexpected, loud or unfamiliar noises in particular could upset him and he might be considered dangerous in this state if his first reaction is to turn and run, regardless of who or what is on his back or in the way. A horse like this will need considerable time, patience and a very experienced owner who is able to regularly reassure him that the human is in charge of the 'watch' and that he can step down and relax. A less experienced owner or rider may not understand his natural behaviour and the reasons behind it, punishing the horse when he is seen to 'misbehave', which of course will only make his insecurity worse. Although a horse like this will undoubtedly make for a less pleasant and on occasion dangerous ride for you, punishing him for having a natural reaction is not only unfair but cruel.

As a rider, you can do your own bit not to try and dampen his instinct altogether, but to make your horse feel calmer and more at ease whilst out riding and therefore less likely to take fright.

The first step as we've discussed is trying if possible to match the energetic nature of the rider with that of the horse. If, for example, you are a nervous rider, a partnership with a highly strung horse is not likely to be a fruitful one and could potentially prove to be extremely dangerous.

This type of horse will feel an overwhelming urge to protect the rest of the horses in his yard – and you, if you are not the strong, dominant type. His instinct tells him that the best way of doing this is to take immediate avoiding action should any potential threat present itself – hence the shying and bolting. He will continue to feel insecure and so will endeavour to take charge unless you can convey to him by using a calm but authoritative voice that you are in control.

A confident rider who can do this will bring an air of serenity with them into the yard. Their quiet manner in assuredly and unhurriedly grooming and tacking up the horse will ensure that both horse and rider are then already well on the way to relaxing and actually enjoying the ride or schooling session, and the horse will not be expecting to get attacked every second of the way. This rider will also be able to recognise their horse's signals so that if he does stop dead, having been startled by an unrecognised sound, they will not try to shush him on and pressurise him into ignoring his instinct, but will instead sit quietly and calmly, allowing him to process the information. Although the horse's body will automatically be tense for a few seconds, he will then feel his 'in charge' rider's presence and hear his voice, which will reassure him, and he'll be much more likely to react less violently and simply move off again.

This process of learning through a deliberate and gradual introduction of unfamiliar sounds, with the support of an understanding rider, should find the horse slowly becoming more and more relaxed when being ridden out and less reactive.

tip

Work with your horse's nervousness. If your horse has spooked for what seems to be no reason at all, turn him around and ride him past the same spot. If it is something visual which has caused him to become unsettled, riding past it a few times backwards and forwards will allow him to view it from different eyes and therefore a different perspective. If, however, he seems to be quite happy walking past it a second time, it may well have been a sudden sound which has spooked him, rather than an object. In either case, it is important that he is made aware that nothing is threatening him and that he begins to relax. Otherwise, you may find that he will begin to spook at this same spot each time you pass it, which is no fun for either horse or rider.

Hearing distraction at shows

The varying and often unusual sounds that your horse hears at shows may be enough to make him upset and agitated. The murmur of the crowd, applause, the commentator's voice, the ring bell and music can sometimes be unsettling, particularly to a young horse and can affect his performance in the ring. If this is a problem you're experiencing, then equine ear plugs could be the answer. These simply block out the more high-frequency noises, so that the horse can still hear sounds on a human level. However, it should be stressed that these should only ever be used during a show and not on a regular basis, as it is unfair to dull the horse's natural hearing ability and can cause rubbing and warts. Consult your vet about the best way to use them.

The human voice

The rider's voice is considered to be an important aid. The horse can indeed pick up on our vocal frequency, which is particularly important when you're trying to calm him. However, what we humans are dreadful at is hiding any form of emotion from our voice. So, you may in the past have become frustrated when your horse is acting particularly nervously or is over-excitable and you have tried to calm him but to no avail. This often happens to nervous riders who try to fool their horse into thinking they're calm and in control. Have you considered that your voice itself may not have been calm and reassuring to his ears? Any change in pitch, any slight wavering will immediately be transmitted to the horse who will then translate your vocal signals into a message that you don't feel safe and that you're not in control. In many instances, this will result in his turning tail and bolting. He is not deliberately ignoring you, he's not misbehaving and he's not trying to throw you off. On the contrary, he is simply misinterpreting what you are saying (or perhaps more accurately, he is correctly interpreting your nervous voice and body language despite your best endeavours) and is trying to protect the pair of you in the only way he knows how.

fact

A horse can detect sound-expressed emotions in a human's voice when the speaker gets scared or excited.

tip

Always speak in a calm voice, even when your emotions are running wild, that way the horse will remain calm also.

The calming influence of the human voice

Like many other animals (I'm thinking sheepdogs in particular here), there is some suggestion that horses can recognise specific vocal sounds, and therefore words, if they are used consistently over a period of time when asking for a particular response. Although a horse is very much an animal ruled by his instinct, we've learned that he can, over time, understand messages given in lessons and react appropriately. The voice *is* therefore an extremely important aid, but is one which we must learn to control in order for it to be effective in teaching our horse and altering his emotions. If you find yourself in a situation where your horse is either afraid, nervous or over-excited and you want him to calm down and listen to you, remember it is likely that you are probably not calm yourself at that moment. Is your heart racing and has your breathing quickened? Then your voice is not ready to be used as a calming measure.

Shouting angrily or excitedly is unlikely to bring about a positive reaction and a steady, calm and clear voice can only be achieved by relaxing your own body, steadying your breathing and distancing yourself from any extreme emotion which you may be feeling at that time. If you can, take three deep breaths in and out and then, as you're breathing out on the final time, speak slowly to him. Continue to take deep breaths and only speak as you are breathing out, which will make your voice stronger and lower.

Horses can pick up on vocal sounds from the handler and translate them into a command.

Remember too that horses are able to associate some individual sounds with a positive or negative memory. A good example here was when I was working with a horse who was occasionally taken hunting. As we were quietly focusing on a specific aspect of his training, the distant sound of the huntsman's horn drifted over to us on the breeze. Although it was barely audible to me or my client, the horse's ears immediately pricked up, his head shot up and he stared off into the distance and started snorting and pawing the ground. He obviously recognised the sound of the horn, was able to associate it with the excitement he experienced on the hunting field and responded accordingly.

This last piece of insight could prove important to handlers who regularly deal with highly strung or nervous horses such as those who compete in racing, eventing or show jumping at a senior level. If the human voice cannot be relied upon to be used in isolation as an effective calming tool in a particular instance, employing a particular sound (if one can be identified) that the horse both remembers hearing regularly and associates with being in a calm, reassured state, could prove useful. In the stable or when being boxed, this could perhaps be a piece of soothing, quiet music, or when out riding, perhaps something as basic as a low, prolonged whistle.

Vocal commands versus body language

Studies from Hare et al., 2002, suggests that horses are able to pick up either intentional or unintentional signals given off by the handler during lungeing, reacting more to these than to the vocal commands given. It is also suggested that this ability has been developed over thousands of years as horses became more domesticated and interacted more fully with humans.

Again, you may not realise that you are contradicting yourself, giving your horse a verbal command whilst your body could be saying something completely different. If the animal then reacts to this unintentional signal, you might interpret that action as disobedience and punish him as a result, causing no end of confusion and mistrust.

Negative and positive sound reinforcement

Negative sound-conditioned behaviour

As a handler, you need to be very careful that you are not reinforcing negative, conditioned behaviours in your horse. For example, say that he is stabled in the fourth stable away from the feed store. At some point, early on in your relationship, he saw that you were feeding the other three horses first and became impatient (possibly worried that he wouldn't be fed) and began kicking the door. Of course, you wouldn't want any damage to the door or for the other horses to become upset, so you may from that point on have decided to feed him first, rather than risk any unpleasantness. What precisely has this message told him? That by kicking the door you'll give him what he wants – and quickly. He can, in fact, bully you effectively.

As we know, horses can anticipate results from sound alone, so if he hears you in the feed store or even if he hears buckets being banged about, he may begin to anticipate being fed, wants to be fed quickly and so understandably, begins to kick the door.

This sort of behaviour in a yard is completely unacceptable – yet it is we humans who inadvertently trigger it.

Positive sound-conditioned behaviour

Rosales-Ruiz and Ferguson in their article: 'Loading the problem loader: the effects of target training and shaping on trailer-loading behaviour of horses', 2001, explored the idea of positive reinforcement for horses with a specific behavioural problem – in this instance, being boxed. These tests involved training the horse to touch a target with his nose, with the target then moved gradually further into the trailer, to encourage the horse to experience moving into the box.

Five mares who had previously been forced into trailers with whips and/or ropes were used as subjects.

The experiments began by positive conditioning – making a sound using a clicking device and then rewarding the horse with treats, immediately afterwards. Very quickly, the mares began to associate the sound of the clicker to mean they were going to receive a treat.

Then, the horses began to learn that by touching a specific target with their nose, a clicking noise would be made and of course, they'd receive that treat. The clicking noise was eventually supplemented by the verbal command 'touch'.

The target was gradually moved into the trailer, with different trailers and handlers being used, until with small adjustments and variations according to the preferred needs of each individual horse, the mares became more confident that the experience was now a pleasant, rather than a frightening one – a powerful example of how sound can act as a positive reinforcement in training.

tip

Before you box or trailer your horse, pick out his feet to make sure that there are no sharp or hard stones in the bottom of the hoof that will cause him discomfort and may even make him difficult to load. Remember, you may have a long drive ahead of you and you want a sound and happy horse coming off the trailer – not one with painful hooves!

Music can have a negative affect

Believe it or not, music too can have a profound effect on a horse. Very often, I drive out to a client's yard to find stable hands cheerily mucking out or going about their routine tasks with pop music blaring from a nearby radio.

fact

It was found that acoustic noise could decrease foraging efficiency in animals; we have to consider, therefore, whether playing music such as rap or heavy metal in a stable is appropriate to a horse's wellbeing and his emotions.

Now, that isn't to say that I drift about in a world of classical music! Like most people, I enjoy many types of music but some songs will simply make my head pound. When this happens, I'm able to remove myself from the environment, ask for it to be turned down or indeed switch it off. But what about the poor horse with his even more sensitive hearing, who is made to suffer the infernal din day after day without being able to escape it? 'Negative' sounds such as these have been shown to have a profound negative effect on horses. You can feel this for yourself if you've perhaps had noisy neighbours playing loud music into the early hours each night or you live close to a pub or club which enjoys deafening those around them. No doubt you'll turn the television up, put headphones on, move to a quieter part of the house or stuff your head under the pillows to escape it. You'll be cross, frustrated and bad tempered, right? Even more so if you begin to develop headaches which can bring about nausea and tiredness. It is no different for the horse, except he can't tell you to turn the thing off.

Inside a stable block for horses at an international show, here they have to cope with the stresses of so many different sounds.

Music therapy

Research on humans has certainly shown that music therapy can have a significant physical effect. It has the ability to reduce anxiety, lower stress levels, reduce pain, lower blood pressure and respiratory rates relatively quickly.

Research carried out on animals however, has been less extensive to date. Some studies have taken place to ascertain whether playing classical music in particular to animals and birds of various species has any physiological effect. With dogs in particular, it was shown to increase their periods of rest and relaxation.

Colorado State University is about to embark on a series of tests to discover whether classical music played in veterinary centres will help to relax cats and allow them to be treated faster under much reduced stress levels. If the results are similar to those carried out in earlier tests, this could have a significant impact on the way we work with horses, too.

That isn't to say that if we aren't a classical music fan, we have to endure hours of Bach and Mozart for the sake of our horses. However, wouldn't it at least be worth playing a variety of softer, soothing music to gauge the reaction of our horse? Particularly when he is feeling stressed, anxious or over excited? Try this too if you can when you're attending competitions, whilst he's standing around and accompany it with a soothing stroke or massage to see if it affects his performance. You might benefit from it too, with the music helping you to calm down and relax which, as we already know, will also help your horse to relax.

The ears reflect emotions

Of course, the horse doesn't only use his ears to hear but also to display whatever emotion he is feeling at that time by their pertinent positioning (a trait that is reflected in many mammals including cats and dogs) and we as humans learn to interpret these positions at a very early age.

- Pointed forward – the horse is alert and interested in what is going on around him.

- Pointing to the side and slightly droopy: he's relaxed and sleepy.

- Pointing backwards: he's feeling ill, bored or generally out of sorts.

- Flat back against his head: beware. This is a sign that he is feeling angry, defensive and aggressive.

I'm fairly confident that as a horse owner or rider, you're well aware of these signs and what they mean (if only humans were able to demonstrate their emotions so easily!) However, do you respect what your horse is telling you?

Many times I have seen humans approach a horse in a yard who has his ears pinned firmly back against his head. He can't make the message any clearer: 'I don't want to interact with you, I don't want to be around you, leave me alone'. Unfortunately, these humans time and again ignore what he's saying and put their hand out to stroke his nose, often resulting in a bite or the sudden swivelling of his hindquarters as he lines them up to be kicked. The result? Often a sore human and a punished horse!

Equally often, I'll bet you've seen (particularly in riding schools), a pony being literally dragged out of a box with the reins at full stretch and his ears pointing backwards. Usually, stable hands laugh and proclaim that he's just being lazy. Have they ever thought that perhaps he's not feeling well at that particular time or, more likely, he's bored stiff with plodding around the same track several times each day with a young child on his back? This 'lazy pony' could in fact transform into a little star if only the course of the lessons was varied each time or he was given an opportunity to learn something new? If you have a job which you consider to be particularly mundane or repetitive, how do you greet each working morning? Do you drag yourself out of bed at the last minute and reluctantly set off for work or are you up with the larks, eager and excited to do your best at filling in the same forms or repeating the same thing over the telephone? What effect would it have on you if you were to be constantly challenged and taught something new each week?

My point here is that it's all well and good being able to translate the obvious signs of a horse's communication, but if we choose to ignore him, then how are we meant to build up a strong bond based on mutual trust and respect? Take note of what his ears are telling you and ask yourself how you'd feel if you were sharing the same emotion or state of mind and someone continued to pester you and make you do something you didn't want to, punishing you when you didn't comply.

Respect is a key issue when working with horses. We all know of the often horrific and degrading traditional methods which used to be used to 'break in' a horse (a term I loathe to this day) and make him the equivalent of our servant. Fortunately, the new generation of horse trainers and behaviour experts have recognised over the years that by understanding the horse and the way in which his mind works, changing the focus of our breaking in methods from restraint to trust, we can begin to build a very constructive bond founded on respect for each other, which inevitably results in the horse trying his heart out for us.

Hearing impairment

There comes the day of course when our bodies begin to let us down, as it does with all animals. Thus the ageing process will inevitably affect your horse and many, if not all, of his senses will begin to deteriorate. This process tends to begin gradually at around the age of five with the horse's sense of hearing starting to become more limited. He will first of all lose his ability over the years to hear sounds at that very highest frequency, gradually working its way downwards until his hearing has become extremely limited overall. Don't panic, this can take many years to occur and of course it doesn't happen to all horses. However, this gradual deterioration means that you may not be able to recognise the deficiency until it becomes glaringly apparent, often at around the age of fifteen.

You might think that the horse is beginning to 'settle down' and mature but this is a misinterpretation. In actual fact, he is simply not picking up the sheer quantity and range of frequency of sounds he used to, and so now does not react as much. Alternatively, you may find that he begins to spook even more, simply because he is not able to hear many sounds and so is often surprised instead by a visual interruption such as a cat appearing in front of him. At this stage, he could be feeling insecure as his defensive systems are letting him down. This is a time for you to change your behaviour around him and exercise extra patience and calm.

If you find that your horse's behaviour is beginning to change, it is good practice to ask your vet to check his ears for any infections or mites. If he is free of any such problem, the vet will probably test him for hearing limitations. If he is diagnosed with impaired hearing, then you need to reconsider how you will handle him.

Handling the hearing-impaired horse

1. Remember that he will often not be able to hear your verbal commands so ensure your riding style relies more on physical aids.

2. If possible, house and ride him out with other horses who he will feel can provide him with additional support and security.

3. When grooming or working around him, remember that he will not be able to see you when you are directly in front or behind him so, using touch, make sure he knows where you are at all times so that you don't surprise him.

4. He will feel more secure if he can have a good view of his surroundings. A limited view from a box is not ideal for a horse such as this.

Positive thinking – hearing differently

Some interesting studies have been undertaken and theories put forward by Japanese author Masaru Emoto. Emoto has released several books including *Messages from Water* (1999, 2001) and *The Hidden Messages in Water* (2004). During the course of his studies, he has found that if either positive or negative human thoughts are aimed at drops of water before they are frozen, then the crystals subsequently formed after the freezing process are often correspondingly 'beautiful' or 'ugly'. These tests were carried out through the process of prayer, music or by attaching the written words to the water's container. The water does in effect, therefore, 'hear' the thoughts.

These are certainly very intriguing results but perhaps predictably, as with any type of 'new science' of this sort, Emoto's trials have come in for some criticism from other members of the scientific community, who have called for further controlled tests. However, my argument is that regardless of whether or not the horse can directly 'hear' your thoughts in much the same way that Emoto is convinced that water can, applying positive thinking to not only your riding but also to all aspects of your life including your own health, has for many years been shown to make a considerable difference.

In an article published by the *New York Times* in 1987 ('Research affirms power of positive thinking', Daniel Goleman), information about new research carried out by Michael F. Scheier of Carnegie-Mellon University in Pittsburgh was revealed. The results of these trials indicated that optimists do indeed handle stress better than pessimists. In the instance of rejection for example, an optimist will ask for feedback and formulate a plan of action to get back on track, whilst a pessimist will simply try to forget the whole thing, thus learning no lessons from the experience whatsoever. Optimists will try to change and improve upon a situation, whereas pessimists, having not learned anything, are more likely to continue with their current state of affairs until they become enlightened.

Although this admittedly sounds more of a spiritual than a practical observation, it can of course be applied to the techniques of positive thinking, positive visualisation and your relationship with your horse.

If you are at a stage whereby your partnership with your horse is not progressing, you both appear to be focusing on your power struggle rather than working in harmony and you're thinking of selling the horse on, stop for a moment and consider your own frame of mind when you're working with him. Have you learned from any mistakes in the past which you can take forward as part of the new 'solution'? Are you approaching your riding with the view that this partnership can be saved and that there is a great deal of potential? If not, and you've long since been resigned to the fact that this equine and you will be at loggerheads until the end of days, then it may be that your horse can 'hear' your negative thoughts and has also thrown in the towel.

Why not try sending him positive visual images of the pair of you enjoying a peaceful hack together or cantering around the ring after winning a competition? Convince yourself that this is only an awkward phase that you can both learn how to work through in order to become a strong team, and you never know, you could convince him too! Isn't it worth a try at least?

As with all of your horse's senses, it simply takes time and patience to understand the true function of his ears and how his hearing has a significant impact on his emotions, which in turn will affect both the way he interacts with you and his overall performance. Understand how his enhanced hearing ability can support your partnership, rather than being a nuisance and appreciate that his resulting actions based on sounds are instinctive, rather than planned out.

In this way, you will become a more sensitive, balanced rider, in tune with your horse's emotions and frame of mind. This, I believe, will inevitably lead to improved performance from both of you.

chapter eight

HOW OUR OWN EMOTIONS AFFECT OUR HORSES

Before we draw together the information you've hopefully learned and digested in this book, I'd like to give you some startling and appalling statistics.

In 2007, there were around 170,000 unwanted horses in the US alone.

According to the Unwanted Horse Coalition who researched these statistics, the number of unwanted horses has risen every year since then, due principally to a number of recurring reasons:

- Owners are no longer able to afford the costs associated with keeping a horse.

- The horse is old or has an injury and can no longer be ridden.

- The owner has lost interest in riding.

- The horse is considered unmanageable.

- The owner has less time to spend with the horse.

- Family circumstances have changed.

- The child has outgrown the horse and moved away from home.

Even looking beyond the dozens of dreadful abuse and neglect cases that we hear about each year (and the thousands of others which we never hear about), just think about the number of horses who are put up for sale by private owners or riding schools annually across the globe, who cite any one of the recurring reasons listed above. Would you agree it must run into hundreds of thousands? Now think about how many horses you know who were brought into a yard or a family as a youngster and spent the rest of their days there. Chances are, there'll be a substantial difference in the numbers.

It is common for many families and riders to buy a pony which is eventually outgrown and sold on. In some instances, we make a mistake and take on a horse which doesn't match our own temperament or riding skills and we pass him on to a potentially equally inexperienced rider, complete with a set of newly learned vices. The new owner finds that they simply don't gel and the horse is sold on again and so the circle continues to turn. As a result, a horse can find himself in a number of different homes throughout his lifetime, unable to forge a bond built on mutual understanding, unable to relax and feel secure and unable to feel truly content. It is likely that not one of his owners has mistreated him or meant him any harm, but unless he is spotted by an experienced and sympathetic owner, he will continue to be passed around this unfortunate circle for most of his life.

But what has this got to do with how our emotions affect the horse whilst we have him?

If you've ever studied psychology or sociology, you will no doubt have heard of Maslow's hierarchy of needs (Figure 9).

Maslow's hierarchy of needs

Physiological needs

In the wild, the horse's physiological needs are those basic necessities he requires in order to survive and to which his instincts are strongly connected. Food, water, sleep, eliminating waste, avoiding pain and to repro-

Figure 9. Maslow's hierarchy of needs (diagram redrawn by Carole Vincer)

duce – these are all present in each and every horse, wild or domestic and these are the needs that, as responsible horse owners, we need to provide.

Safety needs

A herd animal, the horse derives feelings of security from his place within his social group and from the knowledge that there is a leader who will ensure the safety of every member of that herd. As the owner, it is up to you to display the calmness, confidence and assuredness of a leader. Horses will derive additional comfort and feelings of safety from being housed together either in adjoining stables or at pasture, when possible.

Social needs

Whether you are able to allow your horse to join an existing social equine group at home or whether you take the time and effort each day to interact with him both at work and at rest, this aspect of horse ownership is vital so that your horse's social needs are fulfilled, allowing him to retain a level of esteem.

Esteem needs

The horse has a level of esteem when all of his basic needs are being met – physiological, safety and social. He feels safe, he has a bond with those around him and he trusts them. This is a horse who is being truly well cared for in all aspects and who is likely to perform well for his rider.

Self-actualisation

Once the horse is satisfied in all aspects of his life, you will find that he takes a great deal of enjoyment from his work. He is eager to learn, is more likely to be adept at problem solving and will face challenges head on, safe in the knowledge that he is being supported by his rider.

You will notice that emotions do not appear anywhere on the hierarchy. As discussed earlier in the book, horses are not equipped to deal with human-like emotions and indeed it often complicates matters when we consistently inflict our emotions upon them or presume that they are displaying emotions which we recognise among other humans and within ourselves. We tend to live our lives, ruled each day by our range of emotions, which can change in an instant. I would argue that the only true emotion which is shown by a horse is that of fear. Regardless of owners and riders who transfer human characteristics onto the horse and who would no doubt dispute the fact, the horse does not feel love, hate, guilt or shame.

What we must agree on, surely, is that when we see a horse grazing in a field on a warm summer's day with his friends close by; ears pricked forward and tail swishing, we naturally assume that he is relaxed and happy with his lot. A horse's body language is easy for anyone to read if we learn the signs, and it is safe to assume that if a horse is content then he feels safe and secure in his environment and, according to Maslow's hierarchy, having all of his needs met. He is physically sound and not in any pain, he feels safe, he is in a familiar social circle where he understands his role and feels confident.

Maslow's hierarchy was originally applied to humans but the horse's needs are very similar, although he has no need for self-actualisation. His hierarchy would be the herd and his position within this group and, if all of his needs are being met, he will feel safe and content, and we are likely to be presented with a horse who is forward going, enthusiastic, trusting and willing.

It is up to the owner or rider not to automatically expect a horse to present these characteristics, but to work hard in meeting his needs consistently and allowing the characteristics to develop organically and at the horse's own pace. If he fails to display such qualities, it is therefore inevitably not the animal's fault, but the human's.

What the hierarchy does show us is that by stripping away any evidence of human emotion, the horse's needs are exactly the same as our own. With that in mind, ask yourself – are you really meeting every one of your horse's needs?

If we return to the theme of unwanted horses, it therefore seems ironic does it not, that so many horses are sold on or abandoned for reasons which, I hope you now understand, are nothing to do with the horse, and all to do with us.

There is a famous quote by Winston Churchill who said: 'There is something about the outside of a horse that is good for the inside of man'. He uses this metaphor to demonstrate the courage of a horse, a flight or fight animal, to be able to overcome all fears to carry the rider into battle. The horse has many wonderful qualities and much to teach us and it is sad that we often forget to see the wonderful character that also radiates from inside the horse. An old Arabian proverb says much about this wonderful creature: 'The wind of heaven is that which blows between a horse's ears'.

How horses help and teach humans

In common with other animals, horses are used to help humans not only to develop physically and mentally (through such fantastic organisations as Riding for the Disabled), but to overcome emotional and attitude problems. From violent prisoners to street children with low self-esteem, horses give these people back their self-respect and confidence. One child from Cape Town who was attending an equine therapy clinic run by The

a.

b.

If you work hard to meet every one of your horse's needs and succeed, you will develop a rewarding and lasting bond with him.

a. These horses feel completely secure and have confidence in their leader.

b. The gentle giant and the little princess.

c. An undeniable bond between horse and rider.

d. One of many horses being checked by a vet after the cross-country run.

e. A loving owner congratulating his horse on a day's work well done.

f. The bond between this rider and his dressage horse is undeniable.

c.

d.

e.

f.

Montrose Foundation, explained: 'I feel safe with them, no one judges me; horses take me for who I am'.

Victims of abuse too find comfort and healing in the presence of horses. A common feeling shared by many such people is a lack of control after the abuse has taken place, the abuser having taken away any ounce of control they had. However, it has been proven that having a 1,400lb (635kg) animal choose not to fight your wishes but to willingly respond to your command does wonders for the self-esteem of a victim of abuse, who feels that they are, in some small way, regaining some control in their life (Bowers and McDonald, 2001).

Equine-assisted therapy (EAP) is a form of psychotherapy, underpinned by the theory that many humans, particularly those who have experienced significant trauma in their lives, are in fact unable to recognise and/or express their own emotions for whatever reason. Horses in particular are now used in counselling to reflect back the human's emotions, making it clearer to them and working with them so that they grow able to express their emotions in a clear and constructive way.

The concept behind EAP is in fact over two hundred years old and began in Germany, when a number of physicists recommended horse riding to patients who were suffering from hypochondria and hysteria. This form of treatment was shown to have real results and its popularity spread across Europe where it was also used to treat both mental and physical afflictions (Spink, 1993; Tyler, 1994).

Extensive studies on children and horses were carried out in 2006 by Shultz, Remick-Barlow and Robbins ('Equine-assisted psychotherapy: a mental health promotion/intervention modality for children who have experienced intra-family violence'). During these studies, children were taught how to pick up a horse's hoof. Very quickly, they learned that this powerful animal would only lift his hoof if he was so inclined – he could not be forced. In many children, this triggered feelings of anger and frustration, which they were encouraged to express. More important for the horse however, the children also soon learned that the horse was more likely to respond when he was in a calm state and not fearful or angry. This state of mind only occurred when the child handling the horse had worked through their feelings and calmed down.

The horse can, therefore, teach us a great deal about ourselves and our behaviour. This was summed up beautifully by Frewin and Gardiner ('New Age or Old Sage? A review of Equine Assisted Psychotherapy', 2005) who said: '... adolescents are invariably shocked as they begin to understand that openness and vulnerability are more likely to elicit positive behaviour from the horse than displays of defiance and aggression'. This is of course, in direct conflict with the traditional thinking of how a horse should be broken and treated so that he obeys without question. It is this thinking, I'll wager, which underlies those cases of equine abuse, neglect and abandonment. It is such a shame that owners who refuse to challenge their own thinking and techniques could instead be building a productive equine : human relationship built on equality, understanding and trust.

It seems to me too that there's a bigger lesson to be learned here. By encouraging our children to engage in their emotions and express them, those emotions will inevitably become less powerful and more short-lived. By not being fearful of showing how they feel, they can deal with their emotions in a constructive manner and become more well-rounded individuals. Whereas aggressive, defiant attitudes and behaviour is only likely to trigger defensive, aggressive responses in return from those around them, a willingness to open up and show sensitivity will in turn trigger a more receptive and constructive response.

As we progress through childhood and into adulthood, we learn that all other humans to some degree have expectations, prejudices and motives unrelated to our own. For some of us, these characteristics eventually become unbearable, leading us to grow emotional baggage and in extreme instances, psychological problems. This is perhaps why the horse is so successful in calming our emotions and allowing us to relax; regardless of our colour, sex, age, physical ability (or disability) and, more importantly, our past failings, he will quietly accept who we are and seeks nothing but kindness, gentleness and understanding.

Emotional conflict

This acceptance of us is not to say that a horse can be fooled by a quiet tone and a stroking hand. Because deep down he is still an animal who roams free and can be preyed upon, he has the ability to see past the obvious body language and sense the subtler signs of our real state of mind and emotions.

This was demonstrated exceptionally well in one particular case I had. A lady who had previously enjoyed a wonderful relationship with her horse suddenly found that he was nervous when being ridden out and had started to nip and throw his head at her in the stable in an aggressive manner. This was obviously upsetting to the owner who had, until that point, worked hard to forge a strong bond with him. I asked her initially if she had changed anything which may have upset him such as his food, environment or exercise routine. Perhaps his horse friend had moved away, or had the owner changed her perfume which might bring an unfamiliar or even an offensive smell to his nose in her presence? Absolutely nothing had changed – connected with the horse, anyway. On pressing her further, she revealed that she had recently been made redundant from her job and that she was feeling sad, lost, angry and worried about the future. It was very clear that despite her best endeavours, her horse was sensing these tumultuous emotions and was reacting accordingly.

To him, his previous owner, a kind person who was in control and fulfilled all his needs, keeping them both safe and content, had gone. In her place was someone who was not in control but was constantly worried and angry which meant that the environment was no longer safe and that he had to be in control and on his guard at all times. An understandable deduction and conclusion for a herd animal, albeit carried out by pure instinct.

This is a story with a happy conclusion. The client was lucky because after a month she was back in work and her fears had been allayed. The relationship between her and her horse had not been badly damaged. Very quickly, on sensing her renewed state of mind, he could at last step back and restore control to her and both of them were once more enjoying each other's company.

'Even the most secure horse knows that any two-legged creature conveying the gestures of one emotion in order to hide another is either up to no good or delusional enough to be a danger to self and others' (Kohanov, 2001; McCormick and McCormick, 1997). Don't you find this extremely insightful? What a pity that we humans often aren't able to distinguish when one person is faking one emotion in order to hide another.

For the horse however, this is easy and purely natural. Therefore, regardless of how cheerful you try to sound and feel when out riding, if you're riddled with worry and anxiety, you stand precisely no chance of hiding it from your horse, who will reflect these exact emotions back to you in his own way.

Although the horse is an intelligent animal and has a thought process and a will of his own, he does not have the range of emotions experienced by the human. His interpretation of emotions is in fact solely a response to his surroundings and is entirely instinctive. For example, he cannot shed tears if an equine friend is taken away, as if he were upset. However, he may be anxious and concerned if he is then left on his own without a strong herd presence. He cannot 'laugh' or smile as if to show that he is happy, although if his needs are being met and he feels safe and secure, he will show signs that he is relaxed and calm by perhaps playing in a field or dozing in the sunshine.

I find, however, that he is extremely adept at mirroring the emotions expressed by his human handler. Feelings of anger in the handler will trigger the fight or flight instinct in the horse. A calm person will transmit the same calm feelings to the horse, who will then be secure and comfortable in their presence. Alternatively, a timid handler will often find that the animal is what they consider to be 'badly behaved' with them when in fact, the horse has picked up that the human is not confident and so he needs to take charge and be in control. This is misinterpreted by the handler as being stubborn and domineering.

Levels of communication

It is always worth remembering that communication between humans and horses takes place on several levels, most of which we're completely ignorant of. Von Borstel identified visual, tactile, auditory, olfactory and even gustatory signals which are constantly taking place between the two species. We may only be aware principally of auditory communication, using our voice as a main aid, but be assured the horse is much more attuned to us than we give him credit for, consistently using all these signals to assess the immediate situation.

Remember then, that your horse may be able to pick up on what you are thinking without you even realising it. If you're looking to turn left towards the next jump upon landing after the previous one and the horse goes on to take a sharp left almost immediately, or if you're not feeling confident about jumping that hedge in front of you and the horse comes to a dead stop only feet away, it's likely that he's picked up on your thoughts and is reacting to them. This is no psychic ability – he is simply able to identify the subtle signals that your body is unconsciously giving off, and acting upon them.

This unconscious thinking forms the basis of my work with horse and rider. I have treated countless riders who have lost their confidence, particularly after an accident or incident. Rather than focusing solely on teaching them how to ride with a more secure seat however, I work on their mind. I don't allow them to focus on worrying whether the horse will bolt or whether they'll fall off. Instead, I ask them to carry out some mental visualisation exercises, whilst they're actually riding.

Because the rider is concentrating on the activity going on in their own brain, they're not worrying about the horse and what he may or may not do. Consequently, nine times out of ten, the horse will begin to calm down and relax because he is not receiving messages that the person on his back is feeling fearful, which of course in turn, makes him anxious.

One client in particular had a very real fear of cantering in open fields, having had a bad experience in the past with a horse bolting with her under such circumstances. This is an extremely common problem but one which can be easily remedied.

If you approach an open field thinking that this is the place where you're going to canter, and break out into a cold sweat at the thought of being carried in a gallop into the nearest barbed wire fence, then just don't canter! Until your confidence and trust begins to grow in the horse, just walk calmly through the field time and time again, perhaps increasing your pace to a trot if you feel comfortable with that, immediately coming back down to a walk if you become nervous.

In most cases, it's not the horse who is simply being badly behaved and has designs on flinging you into something hard and painful in an attempt to hurt you. In fact you're probably sending him signals that you're afraid of something in this field and he, understandably, is thinking that the pair of you should quite probably get out of there as soon as possible. This is the reason you'll find he dances, jogs and shies at everything until you're out of the field. Once you calm down, relax and enjoy the slower ride, then he'll do exactly the same.

Another client was a helicopter pilot who was prone to thinking negative thoughts during competitions. In particular, he used to worry about whether his horse would shy and whether he would have a jump down, either in the actual competition or during the warm-up.

During one particular discussion, the client told me a story about his first solo flight. During this time, he was holding the stick and having trouble keeping the helicopter steady. His flying instructor asked him to look over to the right and tell him what he could see in the distance. As he did so, the helicopter steadied but then began to become unbalanced again when the pilot once more faced front. He was asked to look out to the left and the craft steadied once more. It didn't take a rocket scientist to see what was happening and after some practice at changing focus and visualising positive images, he finally learned the manoeuvre. Much to his surprise, it was exactly the same with his riding. This time however, when he changed his focus, his horse immediately calmed down.

Over-analysis

Head to any library or bookshop and you'll no doubt see a whole range of books talking about how to ride using your mind. There are arguably some very useful tips in most of these books although my approach is to in actual fact use your mind less whilst riding and you'll find that the emotions you're subconsciously displaying are less likely to affect your horse. During one Burghley in particular, I was walking the course with one of the American team riders when Mark Todd joined us. The American paced a particular jump and then stood, looking nervously over at the drop on the other side. Toddy sagely shook his head and asked what the hell he thought he was doing? The American's face took on a bemused look and so Toddy explained: 'Don't complicate matters by analysing the landing. All you have to do is get the horse safely and happily to the jump and then let him do the rest.'

At a different level, an amateur event rider was having problems with his horse – or so he thought. The horse seemed to continuously and stubbornly refuse at fences for no reason at all. To try and rectify the problem, the rider decided to book a course of lessons with a professional three-day eventer. On meeting horse and rider, the professional assessed the horse by riding him successfully over a number of high jumps and wisely concluded that the problem was, in actual fact, with the human. To demonstrate this point, she brought him one of her horses to ride, telling him that the horse was experienced and would jump anything he was pointed at, providing a rider didn't interfere with anything he was doing.

Horse and rider set off around the course and were doing very well initially. That is until they were faced with some of the higher fences. To the amazement of the rider, this horse too dug in his hooves and absolutely refused to jump! This supported the professional's point beautifully. The rider was unconsciously transmitting signals of fear to the horse by tightening his shoulders and flapping the reins when on approach to the larger jumps. If he had recognised that he was giving off these signals and taught himself to relax, then the horse would have considered it to be just another jump and attacked it like he did with all the rest. However, the quaking individual on his back was telling him

This horse decided it was not going to jump; perhaps it sensed that the rider was also unsure of the jump and decided to stop.

that here was something to be worried about and so the horse sensibly thought it best not to bother.

In a world where so many of us strive to retain control in all aspects of our lives, it can sometimes be difficult to literally hand over the reins. We are programmed to analyse everything, particularly when competing, when in actual fact all we're doing is complicating our riding and making problems for the horse. To a horse, a jump is just that. It is your job as a rider to get him into position where he can jump the obstacle as safely as possible and without making him unduly worried. Try and bully or persuade the horse into doing what you think is best and you're heading for trouble.

Remember, it's the horse who has been given the ability to jump, not you. Put it this way, if you didn't know how to drive, you wouldn't grab the wheel from an experienced driver and try to do the job for him, would you? Inevitably, you'd eventually end up in an accident when you should have just let the driver get on with the job in hand.

I wish some riders or trainers would understand that in most cases, horses are very capable of jumping without any help from us. You need only watch them jumping at liberty to see how well they tackle the obstacles. The minute we get on their backs however, it becomes a challenge. Emotions are often flooding out from our bodies and through the reins and, whilst the horse is trying to come to terms with them, we are telling him how to do his job at the same time. If you have a good relationship and trusting bond with your horse, you should have enough confidence in him to let him take control over jumps. A sympathetic and wise rider however, will be well aware of their horse's limitations, avoiding over-stretching their training sessions and causing future psychological problems.

An important lesson

The one message I've tried to get across in this book is the same message I convey to the majority of my clients and is an important lesson for everyone who works with and rides horses on a daily basis. **It is not what we can teach the horse, but what he can teach us about ourselves.**

Implant this statement in your mind so that the next time you're trying to teach your horse something and he appears to either not be listening, or seems to be blatantly ignoring or defying you, ***stop***. Then, rather than trying to fight him and continue with this battle of wills, ask yourself what you could be doing to cause this problem.

- Why is he not happy to work with you on this particular lesson?

- Is what you're asking him actually achievable?

- Are you asking him to do something which is contrary to his instinct?

- Are you showing him patience and giving him enough time to learn the lesson?

- How are you feeling at the moment? If you're feeling angry or frustrated, could he simply be reflecting your emotions?

Admittedly, for those of us who have worked with horses for years, particularly those performing at a senior level, this thought process may well call for our pride to be laid aside for a time. However, if you know that your horse has a great deal of potential and you long to achieve a solid bond based on trust and mutual respect, isn't he worth the effort?

As mentioned in Chapter 1, over thousands of years, the horse has served us in labour, war and companionship. He has given us his courage, his strength, his stamina and in some cases, his trust. What have we given him in return? Well, all he asks for is security, companionship and to have his basic needs met. An experienced, sympathetic owner is able to understand these needs and provide him with a secure home, hopefully in which he can spend his entire life.

Our major failings

Unfortunately, it seems that we've taken a great deal more from the horse than we've given. What are our major failings?

Not understanding his basic needs

Think about how a horse in the wild perceives his surroundings and what he needs to survive. Responsible ownership is about the horse, not about you. He needs food, water, shelter, security, companionship and an owner who understands him. He doesn't need fancy blankets or to be shut up in a stable with little human or equine interaction and nothing to distract him.

Misunderstanding his behaviour

We expect the horse to be able to translate and understand our instructions with regard to what we want from him, yet don't return the favour. If he consistently shies, bites, avoids contact, bolts or refuses, we consider him to be naughty, aggressive, or a 'problem horse'. Ultimately, in many cases, the horse will be sold on, further adding to his insecurity, when in fact in most cases, he was simply responding to what you were telling him about his environment. Did you ever stop to consider that the horse was simply reflecting back your anger or nervousness and responding instinctively?

Not understanding how we communicate

As a species, we humans are lazy when it comes to communication, relying solely on our mouths to convey information. Because we rely so heavily on verbal communication, we simply expect the rest of the animal kingdom to respond to us in this way, not for one minute thinking that perhaps they could be communicating on a whole different level, in a way of which we're not aware.

I find it is this ignorance of our own self-awareness and reluctance to change which causes the most problems between horse and rider or horse and owner.

When buying a horse, most of us will have at least a rudimentary knowledge of stable and horse management. Mucking out, feeding, basic first aid and knowledge of ailments and treatments along with solid riding skills are all something which should be in place before the horse arrives.

I would argue that we also need to have some other knowledge in place, knowledge based upon how the horse lives in the wild and his subsequent thought processes; knowledge about how to meet his basic needs and not ours; and knowledge about how what we feel and what we think will directly affect him.

It is arrogant of us to think that we can have a life completely outside and separate from our horse. That we can go to work each morning, deal with family crises and mull over relationship problems, taking all that emotional baggage with us when we go out riding, fully expecting the horse not to be able to sense the turmoil inside our head and behave perfectly for us.

Whether you have issues in your personal or work life, or whether it's your actual riding which triggers emotions of fear, anger or tension, you can bet that your horse is picking up on it.

Family relationship experts and parenting specialists advise parents that their child is like a sponge and is able to pick up on aggression, negativity and upset. Consistent exposure to these emotions is likely to have a long-lasting effect on the child, who will often play out these emotions in their own lives.

Although the horse has no human-like emotions, he is even more sensitive than a child, being able to identify negative emotions even though you may have a smile painted on your face and a seemingly cheery disposition.

In the majority of cases, when I visit a client, I know that it will be the human who is causing problems in their equine relationship and not the horse. Human pride being what it is however, means my work calls for a great deal of sensitivity, diplomacy and tact.

My approach is to open the lines of communication between horse and rider, translating what the horse is saying and explaining to the human what they are in actual fact saying to the horse, not verbally but through their body language. By acting as a go-between for the two, I can begin a process whereby horse and human are re-introduced and establish a place for them where they can start to understand each other and where the human can ensure the horse's needs are being met on all levels. This is the first step towards building a strong relationship between the two, based on understanding and respect.

Of course this doesn't happen overnight. After all, very few of us would be able to learn a new language in several hours. However, a willingness on behalf of the owner to work on their own self-awareness, self-expression and physical communication will often bring excellent results.

I won't deny it takes commitment. But then, surely when you invest in a horse, aren't you committing yourself anyway? Perhaps if more of us took the time to truly understand and appreciate a horse, focusing on our own failings and working on our own emotions and communication before blaming the horse, then we'd see the number of abused and abandoned horses drop dramatically.

The author with one of his many wonderful four-legged clients.

CONCLUSION

Now that you know and can appreciate a little more about how the horse can sense other animals and summarise situations in ways in which we are not capable, this should prompt you to give him a little more respect and time for him to process information which is important to him. Rather than focusing on reasons why he is underperforming, might it also be worthwhile concentrating on you and learning how to distance yourself from those negative feelings before trying to work with him? Try it over a period of a month to begin with, to see if it improves the way in which you are able to communicate with him and he responds to you.

We should stop trying to humanise the horse, remembering that it is a different species which, like most other animals, is ruled by the instinctive need to survive, socialise and reproduce. In our busy lives in which we are consumed by time, family and work commitments, and the desire for success, we tend to forget this basic fact and selfishly overlook his needs in favour of our own.

It's very simple. By meeting the true needs of your horse, he will repay your kindness with trust, courage and loyalty. However, in order to meet these needs effectively, we inevitably must learn to understand his natural environment; how he lives and thinks.

I hope that by reading this book, it has, at the very least, triggered questions about how you interact and work with your own horse on a daily basis. If you're having problems with any aspect of your riding or with the relationship itself, why not look at yourself first and ask whether your horse is simply responding to whatever emotions you're giving him.

You too can become a 'horse whisperer'; the first step is learning how to listen.

To become a 'horse whisperer', the first step is learning how to listen; this Kazakh boy would have lived with horses from birth and will already know how to listen.

BIBLIOGRAPHY

American Horse Council (AHC) 2009 Unwanted Horses Survey. A study commissioned by the Unwanted Horse Coalition.

Barrett, L. F., Mesquita, B., Ochsner, K. N. and Gross, J. J., 'The experience of emotion' in *Ann. Rev. Psychol.* 58, 2007, pp. 373–403, doi:10.1146/annurev. psych.58.110405.085709

Benhajali, H., Richard-Yris, M., Leroux, M., Ezzaouia, M., Faouzia, C. and Hausberger, M., 'A note on the time budget and social behaviour of densely housed horses: A case study in Arab breeding mares' in *Applied Animal Behaviour Science* 112, 2008, pp. 196–200

Bernstein, Jason http://serendip.brynmawr.edu/bb/neuro/neuro99/ web3/Bernstein.html

Berliner, David L., Jennings-White, C. and Lavken, R. M., 'The Human Skin: Fragrances and Pheromones' in *Journal of Steroid Biochemical and Molecular Biology* 39, 1991, pp. 671–679

Berliner, David L., Monti-Bloch, Louis, Jennings-White, C. and Diaz-Sanchez, V., 'The Functionality of the Human Vomeronasal Organ

(VNO): Evidence for Steroid Receptors' in *Journal of Steroid Biochemical and Molecular Biology* 58, 1996, pp. 259–265

Boissy, A., Manteuffel, G., et al., 'Assessment of positive emotions in animals to improve their welfare' in *Physiol. Behav.* 92(3), 2007, pp. 375–397

Bourjade, M., Moulinot, M., Henry, S., Richard-Yris, M. and Hausberger, M. 'Could adults be used to improve social skills of young horses' in *Equus caballus? Developmental Psychobiology* 50, 2008, pp. 408–417

Bowers, M. J. and MacDonald, P. M., 'The effectiveness of equine-facilitated psychotherapy with at-risk adolescents: A pilot study' in *Journal of Psychology and Behavioral Sciences*, 15, 2001, pp. 62–76

Cacioppo, J. T., Gardner, W. L. and Berntson, G. G., 'The affect system has parallel and integrative processing components: form follows function' in *J. Pers. Soc. Psychol.* 76, 1999, pp. 839–855, doi:10.1037/0022-3514.76.5.839

Carver, C. S., 'Affect and the functional bases of behavior: on the dimensional structure of affective experience' in *Pers. Soc. Psychol. Rev.* 5, 2001, pp. 345–356, doi:10.1207/S15327957PSPR0504_4

Clancy, A. N., Singer, A. G., Macrides, F., Bronson, F. H. and Agosta, W. C., 'Experiential and endocrine dependence of gonadotropin responses in male mice to conspecific urine' in *Biol. Reprod.* 38, 1988, pp. 183–191

Cooper, J. J. and McGreevy, P., 'Stereotypic behaviour in the stabled horse; causes, effects and treatment' in *Welfare of the Horse*, N. Waran (Ed), Kluwer Academic Publishers, 2002, pp. 99–124

Cooper, J. J., McDonald, L. and Mills, D. S., 'The effect of increasing visual horizons on stereotypic weaving: implications for the social housing of stabled horses' in *Applied Animal Behaviour Science*, 69, 2000, pp. 67–83

Coquelin, A., Clancy, A. N., Macrides, F., Noble, E. P. and Gorski, R. A., 'Pheromonally induced release of luteinizing hormone in male mice: involvement of the vomeronasal system' in *J. Neurosci.* 4, 1984, pp. 2230–2236

Crowell-Davis, Sharon. Dr. 'Compendium Equine' 3:2, March 2008, pp. 91–94

Davidson, N. and Harris, P., 'Nutrition and welfare' in *The Welfare of Horses*, N. Waran, (Ed), Kluwer Academic Publishers, 2002, pp. 45–76

De Boyer Des Roches A., Richard-Yris, M., Henry, S. and Hausberger, M., 'Laterality and emotions: visual laterality in the domestic horse (*Equus caballus*) differs with objects' emotional value' in *Physiol. Behav.* 94(3), 2008, pp. 487–49

De Renzi, E., 'Oculomotor disturbances in hemispheric disease' in *Neuropsychology of Eye Movements*, Johnston, C. W and Pirozzolo, F. J. (Eds), Lawrence Erlbaum, 1998, pp. 177–91

Ekman, P. and Davidson, R. G., *The nature of emotion: fundamental questions*, Oxford University Press, New York, 1994,

Emoto,Masaru, *Messages from Water*, Vol. 1, Hado Publishing, June 1999, ISBN 4-939098-00-1

Emoto, Masaru, *Messages from Water*, Vol. 2, Sunmark Publishing, November 2001, ISBN 0-7881-2927-9

Emoto, Masaru, *The Hidden Messages in Water*, Beyond Words Publishing, 2004 England, 2001 Japan, ISBN 1-58270-162-8

Equine Assisted Psychotherapy (EAP), Charity No. 1122575, Riverside Farm, Rodley Road, Gloucestershire GL14 1RE. Telephone: 0776 691 0063. Email: forward@leap-etc.co.uk

Feh, C. and de Mazieres, J., 'Grooming at a preferred site reduces heart rate in horses' in *Anim. Behav.* 46, 1993, pp. 1191–1194

Finkelmeyer, A., Kellermann, T., Bude, D., Nießen, T., Schwenzer, M., Mathiak, K. and Reske, M., 'Effects of aversive odour presentation on inhibitory control in the Stroop colour-word interference task' in *BMC Neuroscience*, 11(1), 2010, BioMed Central, p. 131

Frewin, Karen and Gardiner, Brent, 'New Age or Old Sage? A review of equine assisted psychotherapy' *The Australian Journal of Counselling Psychology*, Vol. 6(2), Australian Psychological Society, 2005, pp. 13–17

Fureix C., Menguy H. and Hausberger, M., 'Partners with Bad Temper: Reject or Cure? A Study of Chronic Pain and Aggression in Horses' in *PLoS ONE* 5(8), 2010, e12434. doi:10.1371/journal.pone.0012434

Goleman, D. 'Research Affirms Power of Positive Thinking', Published February 3rd, 1987 in the *New York Times*: posted on Tuesday, March 15, 2011 7:56 p.m.

Goodwin, D., 'The importance of ethology in understanding the behaviour of the horse' in *Equine Veterinary Journal,* Suppl. 28, 1999, pp. 15–19

Goodwin, D., Davidson, H. P. B. and Harris, P., 'Selection and acceptance of flavours in concentrate diets for stabled horses' in *Applied Animal Behaviour Science*, 95, 2005, pp. 223–232

Gray, J. A., 'Three fundamental emotion systems' in *The nature of emotion: Fundamental questions*, P. Ekman and R. J. Davidson (Eds),Oxford University Press, New York, 1994, pp. 243–247

Hanggi, E. B., 'Discrimination learning based on relative size concepts in horses (*Equus caballus*)' in *Applied Animal Behaviour Science*, 83(3), 2003, pp. 201–213

Hanggi, E. B., 'Can horses recognize pictures?' in *Proceedings of the Third International Conference of Cognitive Science*, Beijing, China, 2001, pp. 52–56

Hanggi, E. B. and Ingersoll, J. F., 'Long-term memory for categories and concepts in horses (*Equus caballus*)' in *Animal Cognition*, 12(3), 2009, pp. 451–462, doi: 10.1007/s10071-008-0205-9

Hanggi, E. B., 'Optimizing cognition and perception testing in horses using the Equine Research Training System™ and LCD multi-displays' in *Equine Research Foundation Publications*, 2, 2009, pp. 1–7

Hare, B., Brown, M., Williamson, C. and Tomasello, M., 'The domestication of social cognition in dogs' in *Science*, 298, 2002, 1634E1636

Hausberger, M., Gautier, E., Biquand, V., Lunel, C. and Jégo, P., 'Could work be a source of behavioural disorders? A study in horses' in *PLoS ONE*, vol. 4, no. 10, 2009, Article ID e7625

Hausberger, M., Gautier, E., Müller, C. and Jégo, P., 'Lower learning abilities in stereotypic horses' in *Applied Animal Behaviour Science*, 107, 2007, pp. 299–306

Heffner, H. E., 'Auditory awareness in animals' in *Applied Animal Behaviour Science*, 57, 1998, pp. 259–268

Heffner, H. E. and Heffner, R. S., 'Sound localization in large mammals: localization of complex sound by horses' in *Behavioral Neuroscience*, 98, 1984, pp. 541–555

Heffner, R. S., and Heffner, H. E., 'Hearing in large mammals: horses (*Equus caballus*) and cattle (*Bos taurus*) in *Behavioral Neuroscience*, 97, 1983, pp. 299–309

Heffner, R. S. and Heffner, H. E., 'Localization of tones by horses: use of binaural cues and the superior olivary complex' in *Behavioral Neuroscience*, 100, 1986, pp. 93–103

Hendriksen H., Prins J., Olivier B. and Oosting R. S., 'Environmental Enrichment Induces Behavioral Recovery and Enhanced Hippocampal Cell Proliferation in an Antidepressant-Resistant Animal Model for PTSD' in *PLoS ONE* 5(8), 2010, e11943. doi:10.1371/journal.pone.0011943

Johnson, A., Josephson, R. and Hawke, M., 'Clinical and histological evidence for the presence of the vomeronasal (Jacobson's) organ in adult humans' in *J. Otolaryngol.* 14, 1985, pp. 71–79

Johnsgard, P., *The Plovers, Sandpipers and Snipes of the World*, University of Nebraska Press, 1981

Krueger, K. and Flauger, B., 'Social learning in horses from a novel perspective' in *Behavioural Processes,* 76, 2007, pp. 37–39

Kohanov, L., *The tao of equus: A woman's journey of healing and transformation through the way of the horse,* California: New World Library, 2001

Lang, P. J., Bradley, M. M. and Cuthbert, B. N., 'Emotion, attention and the startle reflex' in *Psychol. Rev.* 97, 1990, pp. 377–395. doi:10.1037/0033-295X.97.3.377

Lansade, L., Bouissou, M.-F. and Erhard, H. W., 'Reactivity to isolation and association with conspecifics: a temperament trait stable across time and situations' in *Appl. Anim. Behav. Sci.* 109, 2008, pp. 355–373

Lemasson, A., Boutin, A. et al., 'Horse (*Equus caballus*) whinnies: a source of social information' in *Anim. Cogn.* 12(5), 2009, pp. 693–704

Lynn, Debra A. and Brown, Gillian R., 'The Ontogeny of Anxiety-like Behavior in Rats from Adolescence to Adulthood' Wiley Online Library, 2010, wileyonlinelibrary.com, doi 10.1002/dev.20468

Mal, M. E., Friend, T. H., Lay, D. C., Vogelsang, S. G. and Jenkins, O. C., 'Behavioural responses of mares to short-term confinement and social isolation' in *Applied Animal Behaviour Science,* 31, 1991, pp. 13–24.

Mal, M. E., Friend, T. H., Lay, D. C., Vogelsang, S. G. and Jenkins, O. C., 'Physiological responses of mares to short-term confinement and social isolation' in *Equine Veterinary Science,* 11, 1991, pp. 96–102.

Marinier, S. L. and Alexander, A. J., 'The use of a maze in testing learning and memory in horses' in *Applied Animal Behaviour Science,* 39, 1994, pp. 177–182

Martin, T. I., Zentall, T. R. and Lawrence, L., 'Simple discrimination reversals in the domestic horse (*Equus caballus*): Effect of discriminative stimulus modality on learning to learn' in *Applied Animal Behaviour Science,* 101, 2006, pp. 328–338

Maslow, A. H., *Motivation and Personality* (1st edition: 1954, 2nd edition: 1970, 3rd edition: 1987) Harper & Row, New York

McBride, S. D. and Long, L., 'Management of horses showing stereotypic behaviour, owner perception and the implications for welfare' in *Veterinary Record,* 148, 2001, pp. 799–802

McDonnell, S. M., *Understanding Horse Behavior,* The Blood-Horse, Inc., 1999, Lexington, KY

McGilchrist, Iain, *The Master and His Emissary: The Divided Brain and the Making of the Western World,* 2010, [Paperback] Yale University Press, New Haven and London

McCormick, A. R. and McCormick, M. D., *Horse sense and the human heart; what horses can teach us about trust, bonding, creativity and spirituality,* 1997, Health Communications Inc. USA

McCraty R., Atkinson M. and Tiller W. A., 'New electrophysiological correlates associated with intentional heart focus' *Conference Journal: Subtle Energies,* 1995; 4(3) pp. 251–268

McGreevy, P. *Equine Behavior: A Guide for Veterinarians and Equine Scientists,* Elsevier Ltd, 2004

Med Klin (Munich), 'Prevention of bites by flies and gnats by vitamin B1' Jun 6, 1958, 53(23): 1023

Mendl, M. et al., 'An integrative and functional framework for the study of animal emotion' Royal Society, *Review Proc. R. Soc.,* 2010, B doi:10.1098/ rspb.2010.030

Meredith, M. and Fernandez-Fewell, G., 'Vomeronasal system, LHRH and sex behaviour' in *Psychoneuroendocr.* 19, 1994, pp. 657–672.

Momozawa, Terada et al., 'Assessing Equine Anxiety-Related Parameters Using an Isolation Test in Combination with a Questionnaire Survey' in *J. Vet. Med. Sci.* 69(9), 2007, pp. 945–950,

Montrose Equine Youth Development, Montrose Place, 7 Montrose Terrace, Bishops Court 7708, Cape Town, South Africa. Email: info@ montrosefoundation.co.za, Tel: +27 (0) 21 797 9270

Nesse, R. M. and Ellsworth, P. C., 'Evolution, emotions, and emotional disorders' in *Am. Psychol.* 64, 2009, pp. 129–139, doi:10.1037/a0013503

Nimmermark, Sven, *Odour impact*, Doctoral diss., Dept. of Agricultural Biosystems and Technology, SLU. Acta Universitatis agriculturae Suecia. *Agraria* vol. 494, 2004

Planel, H., 'Etude anatomique et physiologique de l'organe Jacobson' in *Arch. Anat. Histol. Embryol.* 36, 1953, pp. 199–205

Pickett, H., 'Horses; Behaviour, Cognition and Welfare', 2009, www.animalsentience.com

Powers, J. B. and Winans, S. S., 'Vomeronasal organ: critical role in mediating sexual behavior of the male hamster' in *Science* 187, 1975, pp. 961–963

Purser, J. and Radford, A. N., 'Acoustic noise induces attention shifts and reduces foraging performance in three-spined sticklebacks (*Gasterosteus aculeatus*)' in *PLoS ONE* 6(2), 2011, e17478

Rosales-Ruiz, J. and Ferguson, D. L., 'Loading the problem loader: the effects of target training and shaping on trailer-loading behaviour of horses' in *Journal of Applied Behaviour Analysis*, 34, 2001, pp. 409–424

Radin. D., *The Conscious Universe: The Scientific Truth of Psychic Phenomena*, 2009 [paperback], HarperCollins Publishers Inc. United States

Radin D., *Entangled Minds: Extrasensory Experiences in a Quantum Reality*, 2006 [paperback], Paraview Pocket Books, New York

Rivera, E., Benjamin, S., Nielsen, B., Shelle, J. and Zanella, A. J. 'Behavioral and physiological responses of horses to initial training: the comparison between pastured versus stalled horses' in *Applied Animal Behaviour Science*, 78, 2002, pp. 235–252

Rolls, E. T., 'Emotion explained', Oxford University Press, UK, 2005, doi:10.1093/acprof:oso/9780198570035.001.0001

Sappington B. F. and Goldman L., 'Discrimination learning and concept formation in Arabian horse', *Journal of Animal Science*, Vol 72, Issue 12, 1994, pp. 3080–3087, copyright 1994 by American Society of Animal Science

Saslow, C. A., 'Understanding the perceptual world of horses' in *Applied Animal Behaviour Science*, 78, 2002, pp. 209–224

Scheier, M. F., Professor and Department Head of Psychology, Co-Director, Pittsburgh Mind-Body Center, Department of Psychology, Carnegie-Mellon University, Pittsburgh, Pennsylvania 1521

Schultz, P., Remick-Barlow, G., and Robbins, L., 'Equine-assisted psychotherapy: A mental health promotion/intervention modality for children who have experienced intra-family violence' in *Health & Social Care in the Community* 15(3), 2007, pp. 265–271

Schmidt, Alice; Aurich, Jörg; Möstl, Erich; Müller, Jürgen and Aurich, Christine, 'Changes in cortisol release and heart rate and heart rate variability during the initial training of 3-year-old sport horses' in *Hormones and Behavior*, 58(4), 2010, 628 DOI: 10.1016/j.yhbeh.2010.06.011

Søndergaard, E. and Ladewig, J., 'Group housing exerts a positive effect on the behaviour of young horses during training' in *Applied Animal Behaviour Science*, 87, 2004, pp. 105–118

Spink, J., 'Developmental riding therapy: A team approach to assessment and treatment', 1998, Tucson, AZ: Therapy Skill Builders, a division of Communication Skill Builders

Taylor, S. M., 'Equine facilitated psychotherapy: An emerging field' Unpublished Master's thesis, 2001, Saint Michael's College, Vermont

Thorne, J. B., Goodwin, D., Kennedy, M. J., Davidson, H. P. B. and Harris, P., 'Foraging enrichment for individually housed horses: Practicality and effects on behaviour' in *Applied Animal Behaviour Science*, 94, 2005, pp. 149–164

Timney, B. and Keil, K. 'Visual acuity in the horse' in *Vision Research*, 32, 1992, pp. 2289–2293

Timney, B. and Keil, K., 'Local and global stereopsis in the horse' in *Vision Research*, 39, 1999, pp. 1861–1867

Visser, E. K., Ellis, A. D., Van Reenen, C. G., 'The effect of two different housing conditions on the welfare of young horses stabled for the first time' in *Applied Animal Behaviour Science* 114, 2008, pp. 521–533

Waran, N. K., 'Can studies of feral horse behaviour be used for assessing domestic horse welfare?' in *Equine Veterinary Journal*, 29, 1997, pp. 249–251

Watson, D., Wiese, D., Vaidya, J. and Tellegen, A., 'The two general activation systems of affect: structural findings, evolutionary considerations, and psychobiological evidence' *J. Pers. Soc. Psychol.* 76, 1999, pp. 820–838, doi:10. 1037/0022-3514.76.5.820

Zhou, W., Chen, D., 'Sociochemosensory and Emotional Functions: Behavioral Evidence for Shared Mechanisms' in *Psychological Science* 20, 2009, 1118, doi:10.1111/j.1467-9280.2009.02413.x

INDEX